Selected Poems

First published in 2009 by
The Dedalus Press
13 Moyclare Road
Baldoyle
Dublin 13
Ireland

www.dedaluspress.com

Many of these poems originally appeared in the following Norwegian
publications by Knut Ødegård, © Cappelen Damm, Oslo and
Knut Ødegård: *Det mørke regnet* (1972), *Biesurr, laksesprang* (1983),
Kinomaskinist (1991), *Buktale* (1994), *Missa* (1998), *Stephensen-huset* (2003)
and *Det blomstra så sinnssjukt* (2009); many were reprinted in *Kringsjå* (2005).
All previously unpublished poems © Knut Ødegård, 2009
All English language translations © Brian McNeil, 2009

ISBN 978 1 906614 07 2

Dedalus Press titles are represented in North America
by Syracuse University Press, Inc., 621 Skytop Road,
Suite 110, Syracuse, New York 13244, and in the UK by
Central Books, 99 Wallis Road, London E9 5LN.

Cover image copyright © Ståle Edstrøm / iStockPhoto

This translation has been published with the financial support of
NORLA

The Dedalus Press receives financial assistance from
The Arts Council / An Chomhairle Ealaíon

Selected Poems

Knut Ødegård

Translated from the Norwegian
by Brian McNeil

DEDALUS PRESS

ACKNOWLEDGEMENTS

A slightly different version of 'About Visons and Voices' appeared in the Spring 2009 (Issue12/Vol 2) edition of *The Stinging Fly*, for which grateful acknowledgement is made to the editor.

Contents

≈

I

II

III

IV

V

⤳

for Lars Roar

I

All This

(for Þorgerður)

When we grow old, my dear,
and the crows come to get us
(caw-caw, then off with one beat of their wings, into the air),
where will our love be then?

Where will this mouth be then that says
something about a broken coffee-machine, rust on the car, a visit
      to the
cardiologist, a filling that has fallen out, the phone bill
or (romantic) about the golden moon
and the rowan-tree in blossom, which explains away all the white
lies, the cheatings, and all it doesn't manage to say about the child
we never had, and that melts together with your mouth in a kiss?

Or these eyes that stare into the green computer screen day
out and day in and that look at you when you take your clothes off
      as evening draws on:
you put the light out modestly and stand like a silhouette with ripe
      breasts
and thighs against the light that seeps thinly
in through the windows from the cobalt-blue Iceland Sea?
Or these hands that write and write, that put
the snow-shovels in their place and caress you
over your limbs until you burn and want to have me
like a force that smashes into the dams, and I explode
cascading into you, into your womb that was removed by a surgeon
in Reykjavik?

All this that we call love—
where will it be, when the crows come?
For they will not take us both together. One of us
will be the first to lie out there on the ground dirtied by snow
down by the sea (yellow last year's grass, churned-up spring snow)
when the black crows come and pick at the mouth,
the eyes, the hands, the genitals.

That one of us who is left behind the window then, dear,
who wakes in the mornings and does everything
we are familiar with—fetches in *Morgunblaðið* which sits
in the letterbox. Turns on the taps
and looks at himself or herself in the mirror: Does that one us then see
something more
than his or her own face there? Will the other face then
shine through the face in the mirror, as abandoned houses
stand and shine by the sea?

Window, Wide Open

As when a virus
leaves the body,

suddenly
gone, under the lid of dark septic tanks. The pipes roar
in the municipal waterworks, someone is opening taps

or out of a window, towards clouds
and faces

and all this I feel as if for the first time
after a strong fever has loosened its grip on my eyes
and ears. Your face, darling: a window
that has suddenly swung open! A childhood
in rustling grass by the white house

and you open your window
to meet my manhood which lustfully
enters in where childhood youth and age
are all equally and dizzyingly close.

Your window
towards scurrying white clouds. Wide open! Behind it
our faces, timelessly naked. Our love
is here, and it is only time
that passes. We no longer need to
explain ourselves to each other, darling! Our faces
explain us: there is no death, no
ageing. Love is stronger than death,

I daren't say, afraid of making a fool of myself, should have said:
Do you remember? Was that Jesus' words or the vicar's words,
uttered in the little church all those years ago? It was in August. You
stood there with white lilies, yourself a white
lily: a bride in August. Stronger
than death! And you caress me now, as if you know my thoughts,

stroking my bald pate with such infinite tenderness, as if I were
          (despite everything)
exempt from all the decay time brings, all the sin, and I swim
like a finely polished cranium through soil, a seed
making towards a great resurrection in love.
Under the white scurrying clouds. In towards you. Up into you

rises my love out of this virus which is time and forgetfulness.
You swing your window wide open: there is
no death! Everything is
as if for the first time, darling. Grass
grows around my childhood house, there is a roaring
in the pipes in the municipal waterworks, somebody opens
and opens taps.

November Storm

November. A storm came and shook loose
a roof that whirled out into the night, at an angle
it flew and fifteen cows stood lowing in the snow.
A hen-house was lifted up into the sky
and sent a cackling roar down upon us.
The church bells rang furiously: the ringer jerked
on rope and cords, from the fjord someone blew
on dark foghorns.
The cows were quickly slaughtered, the hens jumped
around with severed heads: blood and ice, in 1960. I was
fifteen when this dark exultation met me: the storm

like a boundless will through the night, hoarse howls
from the depths of the sea and the wings that shrieked in the air.
        I was
fifteen when a childhood collapsed head over heels, drowned
in the sight of will destruction life death. Drowned

in these eyes, dearest, that look at you when you
take off your clothes as evening draws near. Outside there rises
a wind like the wind then: grows in strength as night draws near,
takes hold
of our house. Your skin shines
towards me. Dearest! Our love-making
evokes a childhood, indeed more than that: in our shining
bodies lives the same exultation of destruction
and the will to live, transformation, as in all creation, as when
mighty dark storms blow through the Universe, stars
explode and new bright stars are born!

November. Dearest, our love-making in thin houses
when this storm of will rages through us! We are
the dark exultation of birth and death! Like blood and wind
through our caresses, which evoke great bells
from sunken cities in the sea, which liberate the sun-ox from forgotten
rock carvings and let him thunder into
new worlds ... Roofs whirl out into the night, dark foghorns
blow: The storm is coming!

February

Our days less eventful now, dear.
We age imperceptibly: I shrivel, become more and more a cranium
under a wrinkled gray elephant skin in the endless slush, I lose hair
and teeth and lethargy takes over from sweet sins.

There isn't much to tell you about now, and not much
to keep silent about, the white lies are becoming fewer, only
the rain keeps on pouring down in the
depressive bushes and gray trees of the February darkness.
I saw a pair of ravens sitting in our aspen-tree
with their glossy blue-black feathers early this morning, their voices
       reminded
me of the only thing we cannot talk about now—that at the end
we shall die, both you and I. The voices were so glitteringly black,
       a dark presence.

But there is surely a bit of nature left in us two, still,
here where we sit like old elephants in this little house on the edge
of the Atlantic Ocean, we see on the television green-white reports
       from this sea which
sucks sailors into itself still,
these tragedies and hopeless rescue actions
in the bottomless sea.

"You old dingle-dangle," I thought I heard one of these ravens say
so mockingly to me early this morning, blue-black in the rain-
       drenched aspen-tree.
Well yes, it's hanging and dangling on me now, most of my
       adornment, but we
drag these heavy elephant-bodies of ours out towards the outermost edge
of the Atlantic Ocean

still, with plastic bags and shopping baskets in our hands: mince,
        a loaf and two beers.

What then? Over the cliff, down into the deep there?

No, not just yet. For we have a bit
of nature in us still: You who still enchant your glorious lips
with a blood-red magic stick and I with my curls, antennae
towards the sky that don't stop rising up even if they are fewer
and grayer for each year that passes.

This rain that keeps pouring down
now in February: The sky too is like a wrinkled elephant skin,
the North Atlantic rain drums on the housetop as if we were in a
        jungle dance.
We old elephants (my thoughts run) have vast and long memories.
Now we bellow, my dear,
our elephant bellows in the jungle and dance the elephant dance
to hot-blooded Negro drums.

Yes, come, here, for I keep you safe in my capacious elephant
memory: There you are
the same as the time—you know—Out
on our car trip in 1980, it was in July, midsummer evening in the red
Volkswagen, yes rain
then too, but I kissed these lips, and I lift my trunk towards our
primeval forest sky now: oooooooOOOOOOO

II

The Boys' Orchestra

The bass tuba's mother-of-pearl shimmering
against the soft fingers

valves, resilience, light pressure, air-
lessness? none at all: a stream
from his bird's-breast
through tight lips, into

the secret openings of the valves (shu
t/open) through the curved
and golden metal, cut

in the shameful triumph of the wide outstretched funnel
over all the thirteen-year-old boys' defeats, a sousaphone!
like a tremendous unfolding of a forbidden
blossom that thrusts its bell out
of a frail boy's body, its
brass around the body against both childhood
and manhood: six-eight rhythm! The boys' music comes

with pimples and longings in a Sousa march
directed by shoemaker Kleppen
in a war on behalf of puberty's right to the streets
in all directions! The bass tuba player blows

his indifference to all defeats in clammy boys' rooms before sleep
        and all girls'
mocking giggles at playtime and the penniless afternoons
at the shooting gallery in the funfair,
he marches now, on the sheet-music here
with fingers dancing over the mother-of-pearl, so

soft against the mother-of-pearl shimmering, so tight
the lips against the mouthpiece. So wind-blue the sailor's cap

over the red
hair, so steel-blue the jacket over the thin
hairless bird's-breast, so blue like the sky
the trousers with straps
over his shameful snail of a cock, in a rhythm
where freckles and pimples are drowned out
by the bass tuba's imperious ore and where I myself

the smallest piccolo in the orchestra, am eternally
held fast in this rhythm which drums us onward
through the tuba's darkness and the piccolo's trills
of light.

A rhythm which still sits in the feet of middle-aged men
and makes every step we take
a steady tread in shoemaker Kleppen's footprints
over all borders—even the last. Even
the last. It holds no fears for us

old boy-musicians. We still recognise each other
after all those years. The engineer thirty years at sea
whom I met the day before yesterday in the bar, the headmaster whose
photograph they put in the paper, the man who sells packets for
making wine
and insecticides, the goldsmith with the magnifying glass in his eye.
        The names
are gone, but that isn't so important: we
still recognise each other
by means of the mouths and fingers on invisible instruments
in bars, in newspaper photos, behind shop windows.
There is a Sousa march that lies over us. We may perhaps get old.
Until we sprout

wings. But then we will get the glorified
bodies we dreamed about, and we'll get our old instruments back:
the snare drum
the clarinet an eternal afterbeat on the althorn trumpet and
          B-cornet and then
I myself with the piccolo up there, you know. And a tremendous
          sousaphone
sings through the heavenly spheres! We march
in our wind-blue uniforms up and down with our feet
on the firmament between earth and heaven and our stars and suns
of gleaming polished brass and clarinets glittering like lightning
          towards earth.
No, we have nothing to fear with shoemaker Kleppen at the head
of a rhythm that holds our longings fast and lifts us
through darkness and light and sun and moon and blows us
          through all
the starry circle of the zodiac! Stars and Stripes
forever. Trrram-tam-tam trrram-tam-tam
trrram-ta-ta ram-ta-ta tam.

Priest

Uncle Knut was a priest.
He was a practical man, but Latin
was Greek to him.
He died after his retirement, he stood
and dug the site for the new house
when his heart gave way.

He was more an electrician
than a preacher, he began all his speeches
by saying: "I'm not much of a one for speeches"
and he was right about that.

He did not really have much to teach
his parishioners, they had their own troubles
with their births, with their love and their death
and he did not have words for such things.

But he had learnt how to repair
electric wires and he visited people in their homes
and mended short circuits and defective
fuse boxes, he screwed lamps into place

and wherever he had been, there was light.

God's Breath

Little Knut wondered what
God looked like.
No, He is only visible
in His creation, all the Earth
is full of His glory,
said Big Knut.
Well then, maybe the fields here
are God's skin, said Little Knut.
And the air here is God's breath?

Drunkards and Crazy Folk

The drunkards, with splendid names
such as Konrad or Adolf, gathered together
on the outskirts of Molde town. Sometimes their singing
was borne on the wind to us: old hits
or sad low-church hymns about the cross
and the bleeding wounds in Jesus' side. The crazy folk too
wandered around on the outskirts—people like Lundli, who had
once got his intermediary-school diploma: at night, he hewed
and sawed heavy trees, the sound cut its way into the sleep
of us children and got mixed up with dreams
about flying over the housetops or drawing up big fish
from pools with infinite darkening depths

One day, his cross finished, Lundli went
slowly at evening in his white sheet along the High Street
with the huge cross slung over his back.
After him followed the drunkards, Konrad, Adolf
and the rest, and then a throng of children: I kept
my fingers tight around the chestnut from the cemetery tree in my
        pocket.

Lundli called out in his light tenor and falsetto YOU MUST TAKE
UP YOUR CROSS AND FOLLOW ME SAYS THE LORD! His words
flew like fire to Konrad and Adolf, and their big
drunkards' lips replied: "Follow me, says the Lord!
And Halleluiah! And Halleluiah!" Their white hands
danced like birds' wings in the air

The pentecostal procession passed the Alexandra Hotel.
In the windows of the wine bar were the pink faces of queers
and elderly divorcees: in his alcoholic stupor, gay

Jens in his checked sailor suit and tie stumbled down the steps
from the hotel and joined the procession. Old Hansen the
tinsmith, divorced for thirty years, with his heart full
of spittle from his own children, took his time, but
followed him and glided in the crumpled wedding-suit
that was too tight for him, his belly wobbling: he followed
right behind crazy Lundli, who sang FOLLOW ME
FOLLOW ME SAYS THE LORD FOR IT IS NOT THE HEALTHY
WHO NEED THE PHYSICIAN BUT THOSE WHO ARE SICK
OF SIN COME ALL YOU WHO HAVE SINNED and from the
direction of the quay came the clattering steps of skinny old Karen,
whose going price was a pail of beer and who knew
the town's trouser buttons and zips better than the cheerful
seamstresses: she emerged from the shack and the toilet on the quay
and drifted into the procession

Crazy Lundli was almost collapsing
under the enormous cross he had carved out
and assembled in the long dark nights, hammering it
firmly into place with rusty nails left by the German occupation.
From far away came deep rumbles, and lightning cut across the skies:
now the procession glided on to the town square and the clouds
        amassed
over the heads of the drunkards and crazy folk, children and queers
and divorcees and women of doubtful repute who cried out:
        "Halleluiah!
Praise the Lord!" as the first raindrops
squirted on to Lundli's bald pate. The vicar made an appearance
in his black robes, and the police in full uniform
and nurses in white took care of Lundli: they jabbed
syringes into him as he cried through the rain and the wind
PRAISE THE LORD ALL SINNERS FOR HIS GRACE UPON GRACE
TAKE UP THE CROSS AND FOLLOW THE LORD. Then he
        turned white

and fainted in the ambulance while Konrad and Adolf
held the cross firmly upright in the rainstorm in Molde town

The vicar in his black gown got up
on Lundli's margarine crate on the town square: "Go home!"
he commanded, "this is a delusion, sickness, indeed
minds gone mad. Jesus did not mean it literally
when he talked about crosses, it was symbolic and
referred to 'burdens' as a theoretical concept," cried the priest
from the crazy man's crate. Then the heavens burst open
above Molde town and lightning cut a path through the darkness
like a blazing arrow towards the church tower: the bells began
to ring torrential peals, indeed the earth trembled and now the
rain was coming down like Noah's floodwater. I squelched home
in big boots, taking the shortcut across the cemetery,
snatching up the chestnuts which flowed in their green shells
from grave to grave

and after slices of bread with margarine and syrup
came the night with its dreams to us children
and to crazy folk and sinners: we flew without wings
over the town, mounting steeply like a flock of birds
with crazy Lundli and his cross at our head, rising
up to a heaven where big fish squirmed up
from bottomless depths of darkness

We Moved the Beehives Out There

The heather bloomed best out by the windy beaches to the west.
We moved the beehives out there by the sea after the flowering
        season
of the pink clover in the inner arms of the fjord:
we came with the red-lacquered Ford
with room for six hives back in the luggage compartment.
It was essential to find shelter against this wind
that never lets up here.

When I was a child with Father in the eight-cylinder Ford
I thought like a child that there were foxes under the birch roots,
        as in the song,
while we came driving slowly westward along the gravel roads in the
        evenings
after the worker bees had returned to their hives,
their hind-feet heavy with nectar and pollen.

When it rained, we could start earlier, then the bees crept
around indoors with their glittering wings and devoted themselves
        to feeding the
larvae and transforming nectar into honey in the wax cells.
Thousands of them—perhaps as many
as fifty thousand crawled around in each hive
in the rear of the car where Father and I drove.

As the car rolled slowly along the rain-grey fjord,
I thought that it would have been a fine thing to know Bjørnstjerne
        Bjørnson.
Father too said he must have been
a fine man, but he was dead now. I looked for foxes
but it was difficult to see the roots under the birch trunks

from the car window, they rushed past and the further out to sea
        we came,
the thinner were the trunks and cow-parsley grew high by the roadside
and metre-high foxgloves with nodding purple bells
before we came out on to the heather field.

It was one of the thundery summers when I thought this in the
        Ford. Lightning
tore across the sky, but we hummed in the downpour that followed
        —mostly
Bjørnson. Father drove
and I sat with the smoker and puffed little clouds of smoke into the
        back of the car
at bees that crept through mostly invisible slits.
When we braked by some cliffs out where the heather grew
we had to be careful not to slip on roots and mud and wet stones
as we carried the buzzing beehives out from the Ford's baggage
        compartment
and up the path to a spot where they could stand secure and
sheltered from the sea wind.

I recognised the wild scent of wax and honey in my nostrils
as I carried the hive close in to my scrawny chest and neck, I felt
the bees crawling around inside the walls of the hive.
The song about the fox under the birch root kept on humming
        within me
in the cloudburst that now came after a flash of lightning
that rent the Atlantic in two like in the Bible and a bellowing like
        an ox rose up
from the depths of the sea and went out over the coast where Father
        and I stood
at the outermost rim with a beehive between us.

We stood like this: Father, and I, joined together with fifty
        thousand bees

crawling around in the hive we held, while sky and earth broke up
        around us.
But we stood in our boots, and when the storm moved away inland
towards Trollheimen, Hallingskarvet and the Swedish border,
we put down the hive in the heather field
and went down to the car and brought up the others.
We had a good rhythm in our feet now, and it occurred to me that
Bjørnstjerne Bjørnson too
had been a boy here and had thought of foxes under birch roots
further in along the fjord.

We donned our beekeepers' hats with veils that fell down
across our shoulders and pulled tight all the zips in the trousers
and jackets in our white beekeepers' suits
so that we could have been in an American film about beings from
        outer space
landing on the earth, a big being and a little one. My job was
to handle the smoker: I broke up little pieces of compressed wood
and put them in the smoker, kindled them with a match
so that lots of smoke welled up before Father removed the boards
that shut the entrances to the hives and the bees streamed out:
to begin with, they hovered like clouds in the sky above the hives

then suddenly one group of bees veered off across the heather fields
while the others settled on the hives
or crawled around on our beekeepers' suits. We stood quite still: Father
and I, out there on the shore by the ocean that August evening,
and saw the bees return like shining arrows under the rainbow
that stretched out hugely over us.

We saw them descend, each to its hive, and stay there unmoving
with wings like wheels in the wind
only a few centimetres above the hive roofs, they stood like that a
        few seconds

before they started to dance in great circles over the hives
and then slowly took off in the same dance out towards the honey-
      wet heather
with the bee swarm following, in a mighty rushing sound that filled
      the heavens.

Springtime

Springtime! Marvellous old word for
mild southerly winds when all the gutters
in town have gurgled themselves hoarse with rain and mud
splashes skywards (and towards me!) from yellow
buses through the town:
Underwear sheets strung out like triumphant
banners in the wind on Mother's washing lines, boot-
season and dams that burst, a biblical flood rages
down the Molde river, gushes out into the fjord
like mighty whales blowing their spouts
skywards then gliding with their huge hearts
deep down into the icy water. Childhood's springtime! You come

with mild winds towards Mother's clean washing on the lines
and unfold the clothes like enormous postage stamps: the
big red or green ones from Spain that sloped
diagonally, where is my childhood's stamp collection?
They are in the loft in Mother's yellow house in springtime, up
swaying stairs, packed away with other
old dreams in the thin darkness of the loft: my water
colours, jigsaws of plywood
and my herbarium with the white wintergreen blossom

I found on the forest floor of my puberty (moist
earth and ferns, thin fingers under
the ferns). Now
springtime comes for real with its huge feelings! The postage
stamp heart (the big one, on the letter from far away) springs
up the stairs, taking a steep turn with a rocking motion up
to the loft of my childhood's house: Opens
the windows in the loft and mild southerly winds rush

brightly towards my childhood's dreams. Birdsong breaks in
and soon I burst, like the old birch
in the garden, out into dizzying green exultation

Earth, Stars

Death. Roses in the rain. Mould

... so long afterwards: I find
a torn off door from the abandoned house, it lies
rots in the yard, sinks deeper
and deeper down in the earth,   It opens

                    at night
              and someone steps in
            or out between earth and
                    stars

I think so long afterwards. But you
are dead, in roses and rain. You glide

deeper into the earth, down to the roots of my childhood's
rustling woods, where your face is stripped
of all masks, your white skull

shines in the dark sea of earth, drifts around
till all your life has burgeoned
in roses thistles rustling trees in wind

Succession

I

The different colours of piss.
The deep yellow
with its smell like honey
reminds me of autumn
at home, Father
and the process of extracting the heather-honey
when the sun screws slowly downward from
the autumn sky, glowing
behind his bent back: the hill
conceals a sun and the smell of honey
spreads across Father's country.
The water-white piss
after some days
in the hospital, like in
skim-milk, mother's
byre, there were steaming muzzles
and teats then, I drank fresh-sieved milk
out of my wooden ladle. A blue-white child, yellow
hair. A thin clergyman comes
and offers me pastoral care in this
bed in a room like this, but I
do not believe in the limited sacraments
he administers, he leaves
embarrassed by the smell of honey
and fresh-sieved milk. He lacks the apostolic
succession, the scrawny one. And perhaps I am
too much preoccupied by visible
signs of Christ's presence: I
believe.

II

I am not one of
those who deny, their Wittenberg circle
of theses, I lie
in these smells and believe. I do not deny
the seven sacraments, I do not deny
my mother and my father. I believe
in the blessed milk and honey,
and that I will come home at the last.

Sit down on the toilet
just after my old mother
had sat there. The black
ebony seat with the tepidity
of her old warmth, a little
squirt of urine, yellow like a glowing
sun that has slowly bored its way into the black
hill at home. I
believe.

III

I do not deny.
Behold, your mother, I say
to the clergyman (Lutheran): the bird-
woman in room number two
who daren't lock the loo. She
who sits like a ball of yarn on the toilet seat
when someone opens unexpectedly.
She bears all our contempt
on her wings, pastor. Laughter.

You are her son, show her
filial pastoral care, the sacraments.

Come, sweet night, vicar. Old excrement
clings to the inner walls of the toilet
bowl. It is not washed away
completely in the mornings. There is always

a remnant, vicar,
of brown in the white
porcelain. The old bird-woman
who is your mother has pressed
with unlocked door through the night
a grey turd, and the one who had the gall-bladder operation
his dark-brown shit
with specks in it. Come, sweet night, vicar,
there is always a remnant
left over.

Hilltop Farm

"Hilltop" is the name of a little farm, as far up as you can get
       skywards
above Molde town, outside the world.
Great-grandfather Knut broke open the soil here, his life was the scythe
which flew in summer in the haymaking season, and godly books in
       winter
under the Plough which rolled just above his shiny pate, as well as some
cows and sheep, and hens that jumped around.

I thought of old Knut when I went with the sun on my back
today and followed my own shadow, it stretched
so long in December's country, outside the world
and up in the hillsides the shadow stretched, almost right up to the top.
Soon we will be the same age, I thought, as I went
and remembered his daughter, my grandmother in her wicker chair
on the glassed-in veranda who said that it rained corn
over her father, golden. She rattled her knitting needles,
probably she meant: he sowed and harvested.

Well, what do I know, where I swing my stick, holding
the carved eagle's head with a light grip and following my own
shadow?
I see a man climbing up on to the church roof
to repair the bronze bells that have been jammed in Molde for a
       long time now.
YOU ARE HERE. WE'RE COMING SOON
says the sign on the bus stop. Here?

I am walking in my childhood. Older people
often do that. That's how I will be soon, just as old as
grandmother Kristine in the glassed-in veranda and great-

grandfather Knut
at Hilltop Farm,
right up skywards somewhere.
The circular bus comes. Soon I will be old enough
to get a children's ticket, and soon
the bus will not stop at the last stop on the hillside,
but will drive up as far as you can get, will follow the endless
shadow
right up to the stars above Hilltop Farm where I get off the bus
and board the shining Plough, feel dizzy
like an infant in a pram with mighty springs and wheels
through the heavens.

   *

But stop! I forgot that we were musical
up on the hillside, and a little superior there
under the sky's broad roof. Now I see in the register
that great-grandfather's Hilltop Farm had only a small taxable value
   (0.94)
when he bought
the soil he had wrestled with for fifty years, in 1908 he
and my clairvoyant great-grandmother Serianna from Hoem
   became the owners
of a piece of land right outside polite society, so steep
that ordinary people in the town lost their footing and tumbled
   down in the streets.
She smoked a pipe
and read Norway's future in the coffee dregs while Knut
broke open the soil and mowed the steep slope with his short scythe
   and
wrote in the Bible with his clumsy fingers

the name of every child "born to the world"
up there under the sky,
sat on a straight-backed chair and wrote
with his back to an oleograph of Jesus and the disciples.
I sit with that Bible beside me now.

People say I have grandmother Kristine's face.
She and the other deceased hang
on the walls here.
Knut and Serianna in a little metal frame: the emulsion
is gradually cracking in the thin photographic paper
glued on to stiff card, flakes
of their faces and hands are falling off and white threads
and spots are spreading on their black Sunday-best,
the silver.
I see in the bathroom mirror that I have traits
of both of them.
On my way down to the town I glimpse my face in the storefront glass
of the supermarket together with tins of ham and posters, there I see
grandmother Kristine.
When I come down to the High Street I get a glimpse of myself
reflected in the huge window of the County Bank that looks on to
        the square:
there I see
great-grandfather Knut, soon my pate will be as bald as his
on the photographic paper, while I cross the square
I look briefly at the spring fashions
and I see my happy mother, died in '99 (but before Alzheimer's
and all that), reflected among miniskirts
and lace underwear on plastic models wearing makeup:
My happy mother on the hillside! Whose grandmother Serianna
        taught her
to read the future in dregs
and who sat on old Knut's knee

41

and pulled at his beard, and who gave birth to me who am walking
        and looking
at the reflections in the window panes here. Who take my place in
        the circular bus:
an elderly man with many faces, as if
the dead were reflecting themselves in mirror upon mirror in me:
        the bus goes
upwards now, up swings and steep slopes, higher up
and lets people off. I am left sitting alone
and this bus does not stop before it gets right up there
at Hilltop Farm.
Now there is aurora borealis, it resembles grandmother's green silk dress
which rolls slowly over the sky.

Old people have crazy thoughts, everyone knows that.
I thought that if I turned round, up here,
I would see my face reflected in the Atlantic Ocean
or the Indian Ocean or the Pacific:
in a little mirror in the planet Tellus which revolves
slowly around itself down there, but—as in a glimpse—
allows me to see my own face here from above the aurora borealis: thus.

        *

Small spruce-trees with fluttering petticoats
I saw them through the bus window, and I thought of
my sisters. They too don't
come here any more.

This bus is not driving back. We practised
each in turn, it was Chopin's deep bass notes
that were my problem. My left pinkie

all the way down on the piano in Mazurka op. 7, nr. 1. *Vivace,* lively
3/4 beat: the treble clef directs the right thumb
towards a quaver F, semi-quaver pause, semi-quaver F, crotchet
G and crotchet A, but the bass clef drives the left pinkie
towards a crotchet F down there in the piano's cellar and up with
       the pinkie,
index finger, thumb to a crotchet F, C, E flat in the octave above
in a rhythmic grasp by three doughy fingers; plung pling-pling.
Those soft white fingers of mine!
They couldn't manage the third bar in Chopin's Mazurka ... from
       the second
beat with the crescendo into forte fortissimo in the third bar, and
       there:
the left pinkie and thumb fluttered to grasp
a whole octave from E to E in a mighty crotchet beat
at the piano teacher's, colonel's wife
with an eagle's nose: swissssh
from her ruler which smacks the white
pinkie that landed on F and lay like a snail
on her beautiful piano under the painting
of the colonel who won the war against the Germans. Swisssh,
so wordless my finger is lost.

Small spruce-trees with fluttering petticoats.
My sisters then, and I was a little larch-tree
in short trousers, when Mother's shining lacquered Rönich piano
(bought from the money she got from selling eggs) came on a lorry
jolting up the gravel road towards the hillside, blue smoke
skywards: it opened its wings
in the farmyard. Grandmother Kristine was eaten up by cancer
at that time, but grandfather Hol and Father unscrewed the doors
       of the house
and carried the piano in.
I can still hear the piano strings play
all by themselves when they carried it in.

Small spruce-trees. The bus swings
and I think of my sisters
and of the resin that flows out of the openings and scratches in the
        spruce-tree:
thick, sticky discharge of resin in turpentine, rank yellow smell
on my fingers.
No, the bus is not turning back.
I raise my left and sniff the stiff
pinkie: I can still smell a faint odour of resin.

The sisters who play and play the piano in this musical
hillside here. In their fluttering petticoats. But Father was silent,
he took me hunting. Out on the moors we went,
outside Hilltop Farm.
Mostly dead rabbits and carcasses of grouse that dangled under the dark
cellar roof, bloodstains on the floor.

But there is a music up there, I hear it
here from down in the cellar. There is a Chopin
up there, right up on Hilltop Farm. He sounds more clearly
in my ears now, with their weakened sense of hearing, when the bus
        ascends.

        *

Ah yes, there is a yellow (faded) book of exercises
from the 1940's: Schirmer's Library
of Musical Classics, piano solo collections,
with neat writing in pencil: Fingerings! With feeling! But it is first
        of all Mother
I think of now, I think of Mother who calls
into the moors at evening

to him I call blood daddy
and to me, so

there are no more shadows, December's
sun casts its short rays on the soil here by us.

Mother who calls into the moors in me
now, white hoarfrost. She stands with the blue veins
and holds a piece of knitting by a thread

which disappears in an endless ball of yarn in there

behind Mother, where she stands framed
as in a wide-open door

through the bus window skywards and calls
to me

Away

Grandfather Hol goes down the hillside
towards Molde cemetery.
The clocks begin to ring in the tower.
The sun sits in his light-coloured hat
with the black silk band. He swings
his fine stick!
He goes slowly down with the sun
which goes away under the earth.

Secret Things Go Slowly

The old bikes are in the cellars
at the back in a damp darkness
or in the loft: covered by a thin layer
of the dry bright dust. Cycles with wheels frozen fast
in their last rotation before they were abandoned,
consigned to dry up or else disintegrate
in wet rust: the secret slow decomposition.

The spokes, radiating out from the centre, invisible
in high movement extreme speed. At night: the dynamo
connected to the viscous rubber, the uneven light
wobbles down the road.
A fine mesh of thin cobwebs has settled over the spokes,
the rubber swells out in dark crusts under the thin
sticky threads: Small dry wings stuck fast,
it is difficult to make out the black insect.

I sit with a photograph of Father. He has dismounted
from the cycle which he holds tight in against his body:
The fingers clutch the handlebars.

Women Who Serve in Shops

It is one of those cold
and clear days in December: the new
moon shines like a gleaming belly over the women
who serve in shops, they are
on their way in this shining to their jobs. It is early
morning now, and in this gliding movement of women
in the yellow-gray shining in the snow is also the one who serves
in the watchmaker's shop.

I have invented this woman
who breathes nine hours each day among all these timepieces
these ticking clocks and pendulums that fly around:
It is such unstable weather, such sudden
changes, reversals, in precipitation
and temperature. Now it begins to snow silently in the poem
as she unlocks the door of the shop in the High Street.
I call her Lisbeth.

Everything is here, she thinks, Lisbeth
who serves in the shop: Everything
that exists is here. Cuckoo
says the clock on the wall
when the watchmaker comes in

and she can go out for a morning smoke.
I invent the other women who serve
in shops: they come out with their shiny black handbags
at the same time as Lisbeth: They are slightly plump
and sexy and they open their smooth handbags, the fingers
with black lacquered nails grope for cigarette packets and
the lighter. The weather, so unstable,

changes, becomes rawer now as they stand outside smoking, holding
their cigarettes with these silk-smooth bulging fingers
with black lacquered nails. Rain is
on the way. Wet
cigarettes, menthol, with prints
of shocking-pink lipstick on the filter.

Yes, everything is here, Lisbeth thinks
as she leaves the butt glowing on the pavement
and enters the watchmaker's shop: Everything
is.
Cuckoo, says the clock.
Cuckoo.

There are clocks drawn up
everywhere her lungs
breathe, it is her
job to serve here: It's nearly Christmas and sticky snow lies
melting towards evening where the traffic
with its studded tyres breaks the ice over the dark
matter, in the High Street Lisbeth walks
in red leather boots in the slush,
home.

The dark matter seeps out into the white
like a pattern in a foreign language, she thinks,
where the heels of her boots
cut into the black depths under her feet.

At Home

Lisbeth in her apartment block, with its panoramic view,
It's as if she was in a wide-screen TV so high up there on the hillside
her face turned towards the mountain on the other side
across the fjord, the blue eyes
are lit up by a starry sky that ascends out of December's clouds.

Lisbeth alone now, her daughter in her own world. There is a father
who came, she seldom thinks of Jens the salesman
who came into the watchmaker's shop with samples from Zeiss
and left after he had fucked her pregnant in the hotel room, baby Mette
she thinks.

When she sits down with her photo album, she feels a swaying
as if her apartment block was a ship on the high seas: There is the
          picture
Mette sent from Iceland where she was an au pair in a small town
there on the island in its mighty sea:
Hveragerði and Þingvellir, she reads from the back of the picture
and tries to say aloud by herself
the ð sound which Mette said should be pronounced like the
English th. Thing,
her red painted lips say: thing, a thing.

Oh no, she dreamt it all, all that about the job
in the watchmaker's shop and the other women who served
in the shop, for this is the only place she is, with her pills and
the slow movements in her heavy body, so schizophrenic.
That was another Lisbeth, a body that was a girl
in the watchmaker's shop long ago.

And the daughter is schizophrenic too, in her sheltered
accommodation,
an apartment somewhere else.
In the isolation ward, perhaps? She dreams a lot.

She looks at this picture, and feels once more the swaying in the
        apartment block,
this is what Mette wrote about the earthquake on Iceland,
the year before she too became sick.

It is as if I am standing with my left foot on one raft and
the right on another raft, and they are gliding apart on the sea,
        wrote Mette
in her beautiful handwriting there, on the back of the picture:
But it is even worse, for Iceland has a deep
rift down in the heart of the earth where there is a flowing river,
and the land glides apart to the east and to the west,
and so new volcanic eruptions shoot up
and while this fissure widens, the earth shakes, there is an
        earthquake
6.7 on the Richter scale right now, writes Mette, and Lisbeth feels
once more how her apartment block sways while she reads
about cliff sides that hurtle down and houses that collapse like
houses of cards on Iceland, and the cows that stand and moo to the sky
out in the fields that tremble under their feet,
near Hveragerði.

Oh no, that was long ago, all that was long ago, Lisbeth thinks,
She can't face ringing Mette now. She takes an extra chlorpromazine as
the doctor told her to do when she was afraid, and rolls herself a
        cigarette.
Lisbeth so completely alone, she gazes out at the starry sky. Lisbeth
alone. It is her eyes, and a mouth
that screams silently among the stars, in this view from the window
here.

About Visions and Voices

My daughter is ill with schizophrenia: There are
visions and voices that don't exist, says a white doctor
who treats her with chemicals.

My daughter is so psychotic now, I am so frightened, Daddy, she
        says, she sees
that they slaughter people and burn the corpses
so that the smoke rises up silver-grey to the sky while the ash is used
for dunging the vegetable fields: White turnips grow there
in the fields, in a white moonshine, she says.

She sees that they administer poison to the deformed and afterwards
they tear the skin off the dead and the skins are prepared and sent in
to the women with sewing machines who make lampshades out of
        them. They shine
so yellow, she says.

She looks at me here in this ward A and says
we live in a huge slaughter house, they slaughter deformed people
        behind this wall.
Outside there are vast forests
with thousands of skulls under the heather.
My daughter has a genetic defect.

There are meadows full of rotten corpses, just stick your spade
in the earth there, Daddy, she says.
This does not exist. She is the only one who sees, she is
so psychotic. She hears someone putting together
electric chairs outside, she doesn't dare sit down, she just stands here.

She looks at me.
Don't you hear? She asks.

*

Today she doesn't want to speak to me on the phone.
She just sends me an immobile eye
through the telephone cable.

I think that this cable goes under the sea, the ocean bed.

I picture Mette in winter, such a thin child she was then: She licked
at a frozen iron fence, the skin of her tongue
stuck fast when she tugged her mouth free.

This eye that sees, immobile, tender, through a cable
under the ocean bed.

*

You are so handsome, Daddy, she says,
you could have been a model, you and Jesus
could have been barkeepers together.
But I am just a heavy turd.
Now God will soon pull on the string
so that I will be flushed down into hell.

But I used to be so light. You saw
that I could rise straight up into the air, Daddy.

Someone has cut off my wings, now
they want to saw off my feet too.
It is the President who removes people's feet.
But first he makes me swim over an icy river
with a corpse on my back
and then I step on the mines on the far shore,
he has buried them everywhere in the sand.

I do not want to turn on the taps in the bath. The President
speaks through my taps.
I am afraid, Daddy.

*

I am a lump of fat, my daughter says on the phone now.
Why am I not a model?

The President has made a coffin for me, there is no room
for my feet or my hands there.
He works on his coffins over there, we are
sacrificial victims. It's all on the TV.
Don't you watch TV, Daddy? The News?
I don't dare look at the TV any longer, because then he is there,
the President with the coffins.

*

Still abroad, I can reach my daughter
only by phone. She is talking about the President
today as well—It is he
who says I am a lump of fat, Daddy, he says it
through the taps on my bath, don't you hear?

Now he says that he won't send me out there
after all, to slaughter me there.
now he says that he has changed his mind
and that he will abort me because I have
turned out badly, such a deformed
foetus

I am to be cooked as a foetus in a big pot here in ward A
and I am to become powder, medicine for those
who are to be allowed to live, big white tablets.

*

Why is the King here? He came through my mirror
and says that he is the King and comes with my clothes.

Why does he always come with skirts from the Salvation Army
second-hand shop for me? Can't he give them to Mette-Marit?
Can't the King take Mette-Marit instead
to the President in the second-hand clothes and ask the President to
        stop
tormenting me?

He always sneaks off with my make-up.
Can't you ask the King to stop this, Daddy?
The King is the King, isn't he? Ask him to go to the President
and stop this? I will soon be cooked, I am an abortion
in the President's pots.

Doesn't he have enough money by now, the President? Does he
        need to sell more
foetuses for medicines? He can have my make-up instead.

*

My daughter is in another country, there is a phone, a voice
and an eye through the voice. The cable

goes with such anguish under the ocean bed
between us.

I play Messiaen to avoid the pain, I have jotted down in the phone
book "The wind of the Spirit," "Music leads us to God
through the lack of truth." "The angel says: Hear
the music from the Invisible."
A storm is coming on outside, the sea is rising
strongly, dark over the island. All ships
in the harbour, no planes in the air here now.

                    *

Daddy, she whispers on the phone today, I hear
all the voices in the world, perceive all sounds.
There is someone who is listening in me, Daddy, there is a breath
a wind in me that wants me to fly.

I turn up Messiaen to the highest volume, open
the windows on to the birds and now I write to the King:

His Majesty King Harald V, The Royal Castle, Oslo, Norway.

Your Majesty,
My daughter suffers under the delusion that she is worth
nothing. She fears that she is a foetus
that will be aborted because of genetic defects.
She has a mother who sank down to the very depths
in psychosis, in a black muddy pond of the mind, when she was the
            same age.
But she is fond of both human beings and animals.

I hope Your Majesty too will think it strange
that she should not be allowed to experience the birds
and the wind, the sun, just because she suffers from
a deep psychosis.
When she is happy, she has the brightest laughter
I know, as if a prayer in the dust
had been heard, there is a gate in us that she opens up,
Your Majesty.

III

The Feast

Mother said I should invite everyone
in the class, even the fat boy
and the boy with freckles
and the one with the smelly feet:
everyone was invited to the birthday party.

Mother's scones and cups of cocoa, they were
for everyone.
Even the tinkers got bread and coffee
when they came, unkempt and with brown
teeth, to sharpen our knives
and got sixpence for the job.
Everyone was welcome to Mother's table!

Come in where it's warm, she said, here there is
room enough for everyone, and enough to eat
and enough to drink.

Come, everyone, said Jesus
too: Everyone here, to my table.
He did not say: Only
for Catholics, or: Only
for Lutherans.

Mother did not say: Only the best
in the class, or those
with good families are welcome
to my birthday party, or:
Lock the doors when the dirty tinkers come
—Perhaps they need food and drink,
she said.

Signals

The moon is a wheel

Owl-eyes wheels
within wheels

The rainbow through heaven
and earth: the circular communion rail, the heavens
seven fold themselves into wheels. A spring
wound up in a tremendous clockwork: time-
machines, priestly ships
right through the universe, fire-chariots

I sleep in my dizzying
bed in Molde, while Tellus
turns round
and round. The moon round as a ball
in owl-eyes, owl-eyes
in the tree that scrapes against the thin wall

There is someone who says: God!
on earth, as she circles and spins. There are
dreams about dog teams down there, who hunt
across atlases, maps and globes
to reach the last white spaces

And there are weak signals
endlessly far away, all the way from within
your heart, almost only as interference
in the finely tuned listening devices in the observation posts
which fold themselves out like wheels
towards the universe, which say: Yes, my child.

Paper Clip

I pin my papers together
with a paper clip.
This is how I order
and keep control of my thoughts, feelings
and bills.
Sometimes I don't find all my papers.

You don't need any paper clips, Lord.
You keep all creation together
with your love.
Your love finds us all.

The Least Ones

Heavy with thoughts after this seminar
with its gloomy statistics about the prospects for life
on the planet Tellus and the entire solar system out of balance
I came driving my black shiny jeep
up towards my hillside
obsessed in my mind about acid emissions, sea beds
scraped empty, and deserts
that spread and lakes that
shrivel and wither like the Aral Sea, virgin forests that die out
and Arctic glaciers melting away in climatic catastrophes.
That was how I came driving up towards the hillside in my jeep.

Then I suddenly saw two
mascots sauntering along the path: Two very small
mongols, happy
they held each other fast with chubby
hands, her in her long
skirt, him in his wide
trousers. I stopped, in order not to drive
over them, rolled down the window and asked them gruffly
to keep right in to the roadside. They laughed with their bell-like voices
and smiled a sun into me, Lord, with these celestially
beautiful eyes

and I heard low words ringing out from my lips: Blessed,
yes blessed are these least ones!

What kind of nonsense am I talking? I said to myself as
my mouth kept on ringing out in glittering words to these
idiots by the roadside.

She said: It is springtime now, look at the grass! And there
the wood anemone is coming just like the stars that shine at night
in the grass and there! there
clover blossoms are coming red
and heavy with honey up from the earth, and look driver! there
the mayweed is rising up and the blue forget-me-not and there
wild roses are growing in the undergrowth right in to our roadside,
        with rose fragrance!

He, the other idiot said: There is sun here, driver, that shines in the
        grass! It is for
the cows, they give us milk from the grass, driver, it is the light that
        brings out all
the grass, the light
that shines into straw and stalks.

This is how they said it, with their beautiful, round mouths,
and I knew that as long as these two
go hand in hand and saunter around on the roads up here on the
        hillside,
Tellus will go on its safe course around the sun with its light, elliptic like
their mongoloid eyes, like their mouths, like their
heads, safely elliptic around the sun. And then, I thought idiotically,
then the polar bears will survive on the Arctic glaciers.

Blessed, yes blessed
are these least ones, those who sustain all life! my idiot mouth
kept on ringing out, like glass, like light in glass and air.

"It is photosynthesis," I said.
"Is that a flower?" the two with Down syndrome sang in chorus.
"Yes," the words rang from my mouth.

Power

First there came a windmill that whirled round, whirled
round and round in the wind along My shores, a
toy for the engineers on the mainland.

Then they put up another windmill that whirled round, whirled
with big knife blades in the wind and the engineers
got electricity out of the knives in the wind: Power

I, says God, who sometimes is a woman, I created
the wind and the sea and human beings and animals in the water
and the air and on land

but not knives that sweep in a frenzy round in the air
and that cut the throats of the birds I created

The birds build nests and human beings set up their white
houses by the sea, the knives in the air are not My work

I God am horizon I created clean lines, it is here
I rest on the seventh day, by these shores

But now there is something that disturbs the sea in My
pure gaze: they build huge windmills in
their hundreds with knives that slice through the throats of
all that flies in My sky

There is a power in the world that is not Mine, says God
who sometimes is a woman, God who is in eagle and islander

Theological Student

When I was a theological
student, I was concerned
about the question whether I believed
(correctly? strongly enough?) in God,

was afraid of losing
my childhood faith. Prayed with unliberated hands
under the quilt in my clammy student bed-sit
in Kampen (and later in Bærum): "So take
my hands ..."

Now I ask
the pierced ozone sky
whether God believes in me. I doubt
it. But I believe
in him. In the God of hosts, the
Mighty one: He comes on the Day
of Wrath, the question is whether anyone
will be awake then, after the drinks and pills. And whether we still
          have language

to reply to God with, after the sales campaigns, and whether we
          have ears
to hear Him when he comes
in the storm, after the entertainment programme. And eyes to see with,
after the late-night film, for He
is an invisible God except for small children
and great sinners.

For only they see the night grow on the planet, lie sleepless and hear
          the night
give birth, in a storm of contractions, to the Day of Wrath.

When I was a theological
student, no one in the faculty (Blindern) spoke
of a pierced sky, but the child (me! my childhood!) has seen
a dusty lorry bumping over the pitted gravel road
towards the barn, two men in oilskins threw wide the lorry's doors
          (like black
wings) each on his side, their movements exactly similar, and went into
the snug darkness of the byre. They reappeared with two calves, bound
with rope, heave them up on to the floor of the lorry. Then
they drive away, slowly
over the bumps, a blue exhaust fume drifts towards the nose of the
          white child.

It is necessary, the child
was told, we must have food: meat patty, calf steak, sausage meat,
          sausages
in the fridge, open the door! Lamps light up
automatically, the face
in the refrigerator door, the deep freeze hums at the top. Close it
          again! It is
necessary, we are told
and there is nothing dangerous about a few little holes in the sky:
all wheels
have to go round
on the earth, round
in a ring: Spray yourself
under your arms, man! Have a dance and take a drink, there is nothing
dangerous man about a little shrinkage in the ozone layer
a little tax evasion a little flirt,
for there is always a way out and if the flirt goes too far
it is only a little intervention, like
removing a wart, man (and woman!). Sleep well, the wheels

go on and on and the earth turns
in its orbit and round its own self, take a pill
then you'll fall asleep: Here it is safe
as in a cradle with long runners, sleep
sleep, man.
For all this is true.

Only small children and great
sinners lie awake, they see the night
grow on the planet and tremble before the Lord.

Yahweh

A theologian I met
told me that Yahweh means
I am who I am.
But most people probably think
that God is dead, just as
the historical-biographical method
in literary studies is dead.

I thought about this when I thought about
the fact that Arnold Eidslott was a chap
who repaired telephone lines and clambered
up tall poles with telephone cables
so that the signals arrived,
that Alf A. Sæter was a photographer
who spent most of his time in the darkroom
where he developed positive images from negative film
and that Olav H. Hauge was a gardener
with heart and soul who pruned the branches of apple-trees
with very precise cuts so that each tree
bore as many apples as possible.

You are who you are, Lord,
we lesser creators are created by you
and we too are who we are.

The Farmer

Boris Magdenovski im memoriam

His hearing isn't what it was.
He is taking a dog for a walk.
He looks at the fields—the Sunday is a bright blue.
As he walks, he thinks about improvements—a new invention.
A little while ago, he was thinking about the animals' birthing,
now he is thinking about an invention.
He has a paper bag in his left hand,
his trusty stick swings in his right:

the stick swings, a glittering wheel in the blue Sunday!
Boris the farmer enjoys his walk in the village of Brezno.

The dog's hearing isn't what it was, either.
Red blood flows in the veins of man and dog.
Now Boris is thinking that things furthest off are clearest—
from here, he can see his wife Katarina who lies under tussock and cross:
the young girl's eyes see him, they darken as Boris
glides into her.
From here, he can see his grandchild Tihomir in distant Skopje
as he plays in the backyard in Partenija Sografski, Tihomir
skips over a rope.

He swings his trusty stick! Like a propeller in the Sunday blue.
The dog is snuffling along the cart-track.
The paper bag rustles a little in his left hand.
It is as if they were taking off, rushing upwards in the blue air:
a farmer, a brown dog, a paper bag with bread and yellow cheese,
        a cart-track
leading to the cemetery.

Up there in the air, he is thinking about his invention: a paddle wheel!
A paddle wheel in the brook for the threshing,
easy to replace with windmill sails—like wings on the barn wall—
when the brook ran dry.
Yes, we have to save electricity nowadays, thinks the farmer.
A wheel and wings—perfect!

They both hear a whistling in the air.
We don't know what the dog thinks
about the whistling. He keeps on trotting,
while the farmer's thoughts spring from rotary blades and wheel to
        Tihomir:
there is a whistling in the air
when the skipping rope flies between heaven and earth
in the backyard in Partenija Sografski, he thinks.
He smiles at Tihomir
and smiles at her who has been lying under tussock and cross
since nineteen ninety-two.
He is getting close now.

They see a shadow fall from the sky, gliding
down the side of the hill.
We don't know what the dog thinks
about the shadow. Boris the farmer thinks
of big birds' wings, and he thinks of himself as a boy
when he sprang down from the barn roof with wings of cowhide
stretched over wooden laths, wings
he had made without permission:
he glided up towards the sky
just for one second, then crashed into the cornfield. He can still feel
        the graze
and taste the blood when he licked his fists.

A whistling in the air, a black shadow: they walk on
in their dreams towards the cemetery
carrying a paper bag.

They don't turn round. They are on their way to Katarina.
They don't see that the shadows gliding down the hillside
aren't crows, nor geese, but men in black shirts.
This is July the first, two thousand and one, in the village of
Brezno, a blue Sunday.
They don't hear the men shouting that everyone in the village
is to kneel down before the Commandant who has led them over
        the mountains
from Kosovo. They don't hear.
They don't see the Commandant hit thirteen-year-old Biljana on
        the mouth:
her mouth bleeds. Later, it is her crotch that bleeds.

They don't hear the shot fired at Boris the farmer,
his bent back that swayed so lightly
while his stick traced a glittering wheel in the air.
Boris falls.
Boris is dead.
The dog snuffles at Boris—dead.
The paper bag rustles in the scarcely perceptible wind along the
        cart-track.

The Plague

(The Black Death)

The wind, was it the wind, the endless wind
that brought her here?
On a ship? With sails that flapped like batwings?

Or did she come in the form of a rat? And then became a woman of
　　　death
who carried a rake and a broom? Who swept everything away
with her broom. But let a very few survive where she got to work
with the rake?

In the wind, in the wind. We call her the Plague.
She has the face of a rat.

She has a plague-yellow face, she has yellow eyes
opened wide. In the wind,
in the wind.

The stench of corpses throws its stink so poisonous so sweet
so poisonous in the wind, in the wind towards us.
The dying drag the dead to the grave, down into
the earth, under the earth.

In the wind, in the wind, the endless wind
the farms sink slowly, so slowly down
into the bottom of the earth.

The moss grows, it grows like a sleep over the country.
Bushes and thickets, they creep in over cultivated fields in the wind,
in the wind. And the forest grows like an oblivion. Our farms
they are swallowed up by forest.

We fjord people here are silent now, in the wind
in the wind. All that is heard is gasps, all that is heard is rattling,
        vomiting
in those who have boils, those turned black by gangrene.
A rattling, and away, then away in the wind, in the grave.

The bells ring in the wind on Veøy, the priest chants
over a farmer from Nesje, then the fire-red boils spread out
over the priest, over his groin over his shoulders, the priest turns black.
In the wind, the endless wind the ancient chapel in Molde farm
slowly subsides. And everything falls silent.

Only the wind, the wind, endlessly it whispers, it speaks
in the bluish-green darkness. Our farms drift around at the bottom
of forests that slowly wash forward. As if they now lay
at the bottom of the sea. Bells ring in the forest,
from forgotten churches there, in the forest sea.

The wind, only the endless wind.
The stinking the crazy wind, its yellow fingers caress
the clapper in forgotten church bells. And they ring, they ring.
The bells in the forest sea.

We who live, we who are still alive in this wind here,
where are we to turn?

Outside is death, outside is death, outside is only the wind
and no one can lessen the cold that takes hold of our hearts.

We dig and we dig in this wind, we cultivate
our desolate farms, but no one can lessen the wind of grief
in our hearts, the ice-cold wind of grief.
We dig and we dig and we sow, we sow
but the wind is ice-cold, the wind is raw.

Who can meet a grief so great? Pungent as the stench of plague
from the dead?

We shoved them away from us, we asked those with the plague
boils to leave.
We look in the direction of the untidy cemetery:
That was where they went, in the wind
in the wind: We see that in this yellow-black death
flowers grow up: Mary's flower, lady's-mantle in death.

Now the sun breaks through on the peak over there on the farther
shore of the fjord.
The wind plays towards the fjord now, the sun breaks through
on the peak over our blue fjord.

A drop of dew glitters, glitters in the flower that grows
over the graves here, as if the dewdrop was the Virgin Mary,
          Mother Mary's tear.

A Song about Sheep in the Depths
of a Snowy Winter

The white sheep have stood on the same spot
since the end of October.

Reports from Drammen say that hundreds of sheep
were missing in Buskerud,
a farmer in Nore organized searches.
Six have been found up to now, five of them still alive.

At night, I dream of white sheep, warm wool in the depths
of heavy snow. In the morning, up before daybreak,
someone speaks with a loud voice
about the sheep that have been found.
A scrawny farmer thinks they must have stood
on the same spot under a big spruce-tree
since the end of October.
They gnawed the bark of the tree and dug in the earth
until they stood in black soil.
He has heard that one lamb was so exhausted
that it had to be carried home
by a tall, serious chap he knows.

IV

Judas Iscariot

1.

He came from an out of the way place in Judea, Kerioth,
where a waterhole like a weeping eye in the blowing
sand maintained life in a few farmers with creaking
ass-drawn carts. Prophetic words sent forth

from a house of prayer patiently built up of sand and glue to resist
the black wind
that sometimes came and settled, choking, over Kerioth
like the fluttering wings of huge dying birds from the Dead Sea—
but sometimes the wind held its breath, and the eye in the waterhole
saw the heavenly constellations flowing clearly in the black sea over
      its head

at night. Then the village comes to life in the morning, the sun
warms even the dead in the village cemetery, and young women
emerge from the sand-blown houses, their breasts heavy with milk,
and draw water from the well. They wash and anoint Kerioth's youngest
Jewish villagers in the good breeze. Then the wind starts up again

and prophetic words rise up to meet this wind which is older
than the world and comes from nowhere and leads to
nowhere and these grains of sand that are more numerous than the stars
when the Lord permits us to count them, more numerous than all
      the plagues
the Lord's chosen people must endure: grasshoppers and scorpions
in our endless wanderings through the wilderness, and Rome's
legions of unbelievers

and the landscape begins to flicker in the burning desert wind
over Kerioth.

He was of the house of David, and hence a distant
relative of the one they later called Messiah.

It came to pass in those days that a decree went forth
from the emperor Augustus that all the world should be enrolled
in a census, and all walked or rode or came in their carts
to be enrolled, each to his own town.
Simon went up from Kerioth to the city of David
which is called Bethlehem, together with Judith his wife
who was pregnant, and with her daughter whom she had
with a foreign soldier who had come with the wind.

But it came to pass while they were there, that the time came
for her to give birth.
And she gave birth to her son, the first-born, and wrapped him
and laid him in a manger, since there was no room for them
in the inn.

There were some shepherds out in the fields
keeping watch over their flocks by night. They said that an angel
had stood before them and the glory of the Lord had shone
around them, and they were terrified.
And the angel said: "Be not afraid!
For I proclaim to you a great joy
which will be for all the people.
Today a saviour is born for you, who is Christ the Lord,
in the city of David."

And Judith saw the shepherds come into the stable
but they stopped at another manger: she noted the names
Joseph and Mary from Nazareth while she held her newborn first son
up against the shepherds' dark backs.

That was how Judas looked into Jesus' eyes for the first time
with an infant's unclear glance, unfocused,
like one who gazes down into a well.

2.

They nailed Him fast.
Soon I will be dangling loose
in the air: I'll get a
bluish-violet head, my eyes will bulge,
my tongue will become a serpent
that darts out in the desert sand
and the blue erect penis will spurt out
its white seed in this wind's
gaping empty thighs.
But He was the one who betrayed.

There is a yellow wind
that never stops in me: His betrayal
was mine.
This isn't how I meant it to be.

3.

They laughed at me because I was weaned so late.
When my two younger siblings came, Mother always had a little
          over for me
in her breasts. She loved me more than the others.
With her sweet milk on my tongue I held my lips
tight closed when I went out into the eternal wind.
No one was better at school than I was. I tie the knot in the rope
and think of Mother: I was to have brought honour to the family.

I compensated for my shameful sister, whom Mother bore to our
        enemy,
by my hard work at school.
I don't remember Father's skin any more: I think of sand
and salt and parchment and brown sweat.
He welcomed Mother and my shameful sister into
his priestly family.
He was well thought of as a preacher among the sheep-farmers
in Kerioth and the surrounding villages.

I was head and shoulders taller than the others.
They had to look up to me.
I was a child with lovely curls, who read
history books: they were my joy
and my raging, and I wanted to save this country.
I knew the songs by heart. They are singing
in me now, as I interweave three strands:
I am weaving the rope.
The teachers loved me more than the others: no one
was more zealous in preparing for the coming of the Messiah
with justice for our crushed people.
They had to look up to me.
I knew that they laughed at me because of my weak chin.

4.

When I saw Him, I recognized Him,
as if I had seen Him before: I thought
He was the one who was to come. His betrayal
was mine.
This isn't how I meant it to be.

They said that His mother too
was a woman with a past. They whispered
that Joseph was not His father.
Then I felt an even stronger bond between us.

I was tall and thin as a youngster.
My voice was high when I sang and strummed the strings: like myrrh
like balsam sweet as honey and milk, said Mother.
It is night. I sit in the potter's field, a black ring
around the full moon. The strands wriggle
like serpents in my hand.

I let my beard grow down from my underlip
towards my neck when I saw Him three years ago.
There were hundreds of us flocking around Him, we recognized
the spirit's wind when He spoke to us.
When He chose his twelve, I was one of them.
We set out two by two, we went in six directions and proclaimed
that the time was close at hand.

The yellow wind doesn't trouble me so much now.
Here I sit in this field among earthworms and maggots,
the wind has crept into my body.
But when He whispered confidentially with the beardless
John and leant back against the chatterbox Peter
I felt the sulphurous wind seep
in through my nostrils.

I was not a doubter. When the masses turned
against us, I was not one of those who went away.
When I came home to Kerioth and preached,
the teachers said that He was an enemy of Judah.
I shook the dust of my home town from off my feet.

I gave up Mother and Father and my teachers for Him.
Now he was my all.

He had such strange eyes, I had seen them before
as in a cloudy mirror or well: I glimpsed a tremendous burst of
        starlight,
a celestial song down there in the depths.
He gave me the purse, I looked after the money.
The worst thing was leaving Mother.

5.

And it was night.
He went out quickly, but no matter where he turned
it seemed he was turning his back
on the constellations above the city: all he saw was his own
endless shadow slithering like a dark tongue over obscure outlines
of paths and houses and out into the dark air.
Then his dog growled softly and the morning cock
crowed in the potter's house.

He knew that Pisces was the sign of Judea
and Saturn Israel's star, he was
a learned man here on earth. He did not see
clearly now, not the sign of Pisces, for the leaves
were rustling and the yellow wind stung
in his eyes, he grasped the rope
his dog was dragging after him, it tightened
around the animal's neck
and the animal found its way over the cobblestones.

His errand was to prevent this betrayal.

6.

I had the purse, a sign of great trust. I saved money
to give strength to the crushed.
They said I took some of the money, but that is not true.
I put a little aside until the time was ripe,
and when His madness erupted, it was necessary.

They said He worked miracles.
I didn't see Him walk on the water, and what is the point
of tricks?
He was not the only one to heal the sick, but He did
have warm hands. I am a fair man.

They said He raised up the dead Lazarus.
I was not there, but I heard he was sick.
And what good is that supposed to do?
The people might believe He was a heavenly being—
they might begin to speak in tongues, and the legionaries would
        stream in
over the land in their thousands to put an end to the madness.

But I knew I was born to share life
with this man, as if we had been foster-brothers
from the time we were held at the breast and sucked the sweet milk
dripping down on us from a young mother's breast
under the mighty stars that shone over holy Judea. I thought:
I will sacrifice everything for love of Him.
I knew I was chosen.

Call it madness, even sickness if you like,
what happened to Him after He'd begun with such manly vigour
to blow new life into our people who had grown so sluggish.

I was there when He overturned the tables of the merchants
in the temple and swung the rope over them.
I was there when He cried out: "Do not think
I have come with peace, I have come with a sword!"

There were women who clung to Him.
There was that Mary Magdalene: "What
are we to do with His madness?"
I asked.
They refused to listen. Peter placed
his huge ear, overgrown with wax, against my mouth.
John blushed in the light that shone from that face
where the madness was plain to see
for anyone with normal understanding.

I asked what all this would come to?
What would this come to, when the money
was squandered by Mary on ointments and perfume
with which she anointed His body:
she leant over him, lightly clothed,
with swaying breasts. I turned away. Here I sit

and hear a crackling in the branches, a rustling whisper
of insects and toads as they creep around me in the field.
But the dog lies quietly at my feet. I loosen the leash
from his neck, it will make a fine noose
and I tie it to the rope with a knot: then I sling
the rough end over a black leafless branch
at which the dog's yellow eyes gaze.

7.

He was not without dreams.
Often he dreamed that he was without words.

An infant in a dark barn
abandoned. He dreamed of the smells of hay
and milk and the rank odour of dung, of horse piss
and the sounds of whinnying animals, hens cackling
and snorting pigs.
He dreamed about his mother's back, turned away,
and then his screams woke him up (in the dream)
and he looked into the eyes of another child
who lay there.
The other child laid his hands
on him, and they shared a kind of cradle-fellowship
and in the dream he kissed the other child.
When he woke, he recognized those eyes
and after such dreams he was tormented by stars
which stuck fast like sand to the inside of his eyeball.
On such days He said little, but kept close
to Him.

He had never seen angels.

8.

I was there at the feast in Lazarus' home
just before Passover. It was Mary Magdalene
who took us with her to her famous brother
in Bethany.
It was meant to be just the twelve us and Him
in the party, the women Mary and her sister Martha
were to make the meal and serve it.
But a gang of uneducated persons gathered together
outside the house to see the miracle-man and Lazarus
after he had risen from the tomb in his stinking grave-clothes.
I felt sick, I had dreamed that night,

the white grains of sand flickered in my skull.
I tried to close my eyelids again
but I felt him move away when I laid my hand
on His robe.

We had had red wine and food, and the one
who to all appearances had been dead
slapped his fat thigh, drank more wine, and laughed
at Peter's tall tales of the blue whales he had caught
on his hook in Lake Genesareth.

Then through my sore half-opened eyes I saw
how Mary M. waved to Him to leave the table
and drew Him down on to a carpet.
She lay over Him, lay there astride him with her round backside
in the air and let down her mane of hair, which flowed over Him:
she began to rub His feet
with genuine nard-oil imported from the Himalayas,
worked her way up over His body, His thighs, rubbed
with her slender fingers and dried Him
with her own hair!

My eyes stung, my head
was like a wasps' nest, but somebody had to put a stop
to this madness and I cried out desperately
that things have reached the limit now, now things have gone far enough,
those drops are costly,
worth three hundred denarii at least: Why? Why
was not this superfluous vanity sold
and the money given to the faithful of Judah's tribe?

White wasps buzzed behind my eyes
and the room was filled to bursting
with the fragrant perfume and I was without words

and slid into a mist there, without dreams,
perhaps for a few seconds only, and I saw
that this shameful act of love did not stop
and I thought I heard Him say: Let her do it,
for she has kept this oil for my burial.

This was six days before the Passover. When I came to my senses
I had made my decision.
No one was to come between me and the great deed.
The day after, He took His seat on a ridiculous ass
and rode like a loser westward over the country fields
the three kilometres into Jerusalem.

9.

This I did for Him
I loved Him who betrayed

One who has loved is never completely alone, I have
the dog

Was there anything else?

With the noose around my neck, the rope
in the branch, I stand with my toes
on the dog. Was there anything else?

The dog twists his head round and licks my feet,
that is how he anoints me.
when he gets up and goes away, there is nothing more

What I did, I did
I asked them to look after Him

They gave me thirty pieces of silver, a risible sum
I put them in the purse

They were learned men, like myself
We had read Hippocrates, we knew our Greek and Latin
He was a sick man, crazy
A disequilibrium between *sanguis, phlegma,*
chole and *melaina chole,*
a rational empirical analysis
He needed to be locked up, that is what the learned men wanted
He was not the one I had thought
but I loved Him all the same

There was no betrayal in their eyes
I was just to give them a sign to show which one He was

In the garden I kissed Him for the last time: the sign
His lips were soft like the infant in my dream,
He tasted of milk and honey

Is madness a betrayal? The dog
lies under my feet, still
Rather a case of betrayal as a result of madness
he looks at me with yellow eyes
like the full moon over the potter's field

They gave Him to Pilate
This isn't how I meant it to be

I was there, with the dog
I heard the people cry

10.

It may well be that Pontius Pilate was an upright man.
He came from one of Rome's best families, had studied
jurisprudence, philosophy and military strategy, as well as rhetoric.

Tiberius Julius Caesar appointed him procurator
over Palestine twenty-six years after the great census.
Otherwise, our sources are vague, it is like staring
down and looking for a face in a muddy well.
Josephus and Philo, Jewish authors, see a greedy man
with a hard heart.
Luke, a Greek physician and author, gives us a portrait of a weak
but fair man who wanted to let Jesus go
after an admonition and a few strokes of the scourge.
John, a Jewish-Christian author (and apostle?), makes him
a nervous intellectual who let Jesus be slapped around, scourged,
crowned with thorns, put a purple cloak on him,
and then asked: What is truth?

Pilate disliked the Jews and the stifling heat in Jerusalem.
He had thin, white skin and lived by the sea, in Caesarea
where the cooling winds swept bluely in from the Mediterranean.
In the course of his official duties he had to sit in judgment in Jerusalem
with its narrow streets, sweat, stink and sickly heat
and stay as guest of the uneducated petty king Herod, whom he despised.
He sweats:

What is truth?—while the blood runs down the cheek
of the other man.

Judas from Kerioth in Judea, of David's stock, stood among the people
who shrieked as if they were at the stadium
and demanded that the judge release Barabbas
but kill Jesus.

The dog gazed at the one crowned with thorns, the crowd of people
pressed forward from all sides with their cry for blood
and crucifixion.
The sand behind his eyeball began to chafe when a ray of sunlight
glittered from the legionary's golden eagle and he saw everything
as if from inside a wasps' nest of golden larvae and insect wings:

Pilate's mouth
moves slowly,

like a dried-up leaf
slowly
downwards, falls into

the black darkness of a well, mud
without language, lost

The mouth slowly in the mud at the bottom of the well.
Judas read on the frog-lips:
Iesus Nazarenus Rex Iudaeorum.

11.

The sultry heat lay like a lid
over his head, Pilate could scarcely
move his mouth. At nights he lay out in the cool corridor

but even when he lay there and gazed up at the constellation
Pisces he breathed in dry sand. It seemed that all life
withered away, the blood coagulated
in the veins of the plants and crumbled into clods like sand.
Was he really dreaming, then?
He thought he heard a distant thunder from far off

but when he sat up he saw the almost half-obliterated shadow
of a man and a dog down there, disappearing in the direction of the
        temple.
A low growling remained there on the cobblestones, he gasped for air.

The dog stopped outside the temple, the man
let go of the leash. They stood immobile
until day dawned. Judas

hesitated a little, took hold of the leash.
The man and the dog went back to the square
where people had begun to gather.
It was Friday morning.

After the trial and the undignified presentation
Pilate lay down again in his cool corridor. The air
was even sultrier, a sour moisture trickled out
from every pore in his body. The new garment the tailor
in Rome had sent stuck to his body. Stretching out
his arm for his wineglass he heard the rumbling
of distant thunder once more
and his thoughts turned briefly to the man from Nazareth
but the wine tasted of gall and he let the glass
fall to the stone floor.

The air was utterly still now, like jelly
and he struggled to get up
when he heard the rumblings nearer at hand.
He saw the man and the dog down there still, disappearing
in at the temple gate. When the first drops

hit his tortured forehead the man
and the dog came out of the temple again, in the direction
of the potter and it was suddenly

darker. The thunder crashed now, and lightning
sliced its path over the sky: the darkness
lay thick on Jerusalem and the air like jelly
dissolved in cascading water zigzag lightning
and flood waves streaming down on the temple square.

When a mighty lightning flash hit the temple, Pilate hurried in
wet through. The peals of thunder made the solid residence
tremble, and he smiled at the thought of superstitious Herod
with his fear of angels and demons and the resurrection of the dead.

12.

For Him I loved—He who betrayed—
I betrayed

Moon sand
in my eyes, yellow
dog

that's all that's left, innocent blood
streams up towards the fishes
in the sky

The dog moves: if he goes
now

the noose will fall tight around my neck

I see unclearly the fish teem
in the constellation in the sky, as if in a
sea infinitely

deep there I sink
not
but will dangle

The dog gets up. I
glide

out in the air

now, I shall dangle
on a rope, I

will soon stink in the wind, my belly
swells out, and Judas Iscariot

bulges out in the rain and will be scorched
in the sun, those eyes
that saw Him suffer for my guilt
will be pecked out by birds, the mouth

will scream without tongue and lips
in the desert wind over Palestine

and over all the lands: His name
and over all the seven seas in the wind:

His name His name

V

MISSA

To Hege
with thanks for her help

Salutatio

Of ashes and smoke.
Death
and mirrors, smudged: a loom
set up at an angle against the wall, in the half-darkness, in the
caved-in stone cellar. Here are tortured
memories of infants. Here are the thin women
like ravens, like shadows, with dripping swords they
wind the loom.

The loom set up is broad
down there: it
presages death, rain
that drips and the drop is blood
is blood.
A loom set up, grey,
its framework made of spears.
Of ashes and smoke, the mirror

unclear *In nomine, in*
nomine See, the loom
grows with human innards as
warp, the loom is stretched tight
with men's dangling heads
as weights *In nomine*
Patris, et Filii the shadows of the raven-women
who wind and wind a loom, a
splintered mirror
in an infant's memory: the cellar darkness, sooty glass shards
stuck to the innards and the web-spear flies
the shadows wind and wind a loom: our
faces rage around like splinters in the loom, Hildr and

Hjørþrimul wind the loom with red
dripping swords, Sanngriðr and Svipul
wind and wind and the loom grows *In nomine Patris*
et Filii et Spiritus Sancti

I was an infant weeping
in the cellar: of ashes and smoke,
caved-in. A wet loom
in the dark, something
is moving there. There are shadows
and the acrid stink, something drips
and drips and no one hears
the weeping *gratia Domini nostri Jesu Christi*
et caritas Dei et communicatio Sancti
Spiritus sit cum omnibus vobis I was

a child in a caved-in cellar
by the sea, lost
until I called Mummy's name and she
found me and lifted me up to her big
breasts heavy with milk: Father came in,
white spume of the raging sea in his hair. He carried me
home with his right hand, close against his heart, with his left
he carried a handful of fish. I can still feel
the warmth of his big body, and his voice
that sang me to sleep: *et cum spiritu tuo*

Kyrie

(Not my voice, Lord, my daughter's voice. A darkness
envelops her in the isolation ward. Hear my prayers,
Lord, creator of the galaxies, not just
creator of the sun, but also of the heavy moon that
tugs the water over the banks in my daughter's head,
God of Abraham and Isaac and Jacob, you
who are also God of the mentally ill: *Kyrie eléison, Christe
eléison. Kyrie eléison*)

*

I am a star turn
in this festival: for instance

I lose my face in this mirror, it
sinks slowly in the pool and moves
steeply, darkening down through clumps of
frogspawn to the mud,
the stench

(Kyrie eléison)

It is my daughter who is speaking
This is a horror festival she says
Superstars well-known artistes: The mirror
played tricks. The face that is stuck there
and sinks into the looking-glass when I turn
my back,

sinks
slowly darkening, down
in the pool.

(Christe eléison)

*

Why are you telling lies
and saying you are my father? Just put on
your white TV showman's gloves. You are the one
who shoots the bullets in my face, the hard-cocked
springs you shoot with, I don't understand the jigsaw
puzzle: numbers and
figures? I dreamed
I was in Paradise with a barkeeper
I know. Then you came
and he vanished into thin
air. Just put on

the white TV showman's gloves: you
are not my father.

Why can't I go out as I like?
Why don't you have me discharged,
Father? Here's my passport.

Why do all the pictures turn to monsters?
Look, here's my passport photograph: why are you turning me
into a monster?

(Kyrie eléison)

104

*

Burnt
to pieces, my face is violet,
still hanging in the mirror: like this

What are you up to, disfiguring my face, Father?
Can't you make me up so I become Pretty Woman instead?

Like leaves, a rustling. There is a noise
of perfume, and a mirror

that rots:

stench. A womb removed by an operation
on the rubbish heap.

Why do you keep sterilizing me all the time, Father?

(Christe eléison. Christe eléison)

*

I am stuck fast in here. In this
body, I can't get
out. A smell
is seeping up from the cellar, the floorboards
are so full of cracks. It is
the Slaughterer who is slaughtering

down there, a harsh smell that
seeps, seeps. Father

wants to take me with him, bear the innards
out to the rippling brook, they have to be
cleaned. It is October, the moon
waxes golden and that which destroys

must flow away. But I am stuck
so fast in this body, in here. A smell
is seeping up from the cellar, raw.

(Kyrie eléison. Kyrie eléison)

*

A sweet rotten smell
from October's mould. The potatoes
have long since been dug up and slung
into the house, but now

a sweet stench rises from Grandfather's earth
and an aunt sits, her legs gripping
a zinc bucket, in the yellow kitchen, peeling
potatoes and talking about cancer
that spreads like branches
along the bone marrow. She cuts
with a sharp knife in the dirty water: November. Grandfather
shrivels up. The burial procession is a long, narrow
movement of black in December's snow.

I sense the sweet and rotten smells
seeping in here from the sick
October mould beneath December's snow. I close
my mouth.

I hear Father's voice and I look
in the mirror, something is spreading
in my face. But I can't get out
of this heavy body. I breathe
it in, a sweet stench.

(Christe eléison. Christe eléison)

*

I ask what you are up to, disfiguring me, Father. I am
girl, 23. I am Silje. There is a voice

in my head. There is a film
racing at unchecked speed before my eyes. I want to know
what you are up to, disfiguring me.

(Kyrie eléison. Kyrie eléison)

*

(I am the one who looks on, Lord. Have mercy on me:)

*

After training on the health studio apparatus and 12 min.
sauna, a steam bath with the heat set far too high this evening,
the blood vessels in my feet have contracted

now: ice
cold creeps steadily upwards from soles to thighs, sweats
coldly. The room is empty, it is a
home, the woman
doing her choir rehearsals
has her set times:

he stands in his evening and stares at girls in a car out there:
Renault Clio RN, 92-mod.,
red,
5 gears, maybe 120,000 km, there is a window, he
stares in his darkened room. They
drive off. They just went in for a moment and came out
again with something. On the other side. A girl's laughter

still hangs on the pavement out there, exhaust fume slowly
dissolves and a grief spreads from his breast
along his arms. There will be a tremendous
cold spell after this, he knows. The Met. Office
is already predicting
night frost. He reflects that he is a father and that nothing
will be as it was before. He has a daughter
shut up in the sound-proofed, isolation
ward, no mirrors to display her girl's face. The blood vessels
contract in his body. Night is coming and there's no, no
girl called Silje in the mirror.

*

Kyrie, eléison. Kyrie, eléison.
Christe, eléison. Christe, eléison.
Kyrie, eléison. Kyrie, eléison.

Lord, have mercy on us.
Christ, have mercy on us.
Lord, have mercy on us.

Why are you silent, Lord?
Why are you silent about my daughter's suffering?
Is it your steps she hears in the corridor
outside the isolation ward?

*

Is it you who are president
of this horror festival? I am

a star turn, a face burnt
to pieces, violet, which sinks

steeply to the bottom of the pool. Frogspawn
under the surface on the mirror, crowds
of larvae on the glass-clear

surface. In there: the stench

of the pool-floor, the life in the mud. I can't
get away, like a rotten
stick. Why

can I not have the face
I got from you, Father? They are breaking my neck, yes,
there is a stick: my neck, my face, my hair
are disappearing. The telephone whispers
that I am ugly. I have stopped enjoying
having my picture taken in the photograph booth.

The moonlight,
there is a big watercourse in my head: I

was washed away into the isolation ward. All the taps are
filling up the pots. Now all my faces are coming:
they were so pretty—there is one that looks
like me, except the hair is dark and smooth. I thought
it was me. Why did she come

and become me? She just sits
in her chair and shoots her mouth off
at you, Father. Can't she stop?

The faces fill the pots with voices and water.
The one who came to take me out
of this freezer and cook me in a pot
and eat me: why are you cooking me

all of a sudden? Can't you buy
enough food? Why do all the faces come
to eat me, then? My hair
is disappearing, Father. I am bones

and skull: who is it babbling
in my skull?

This body isn't mine.
I am stuck fast in it. Get me discharged,

Father, out of here.

(Kyrie eléison)

110

Gloria

Gloria in excelsis Deo. And peace
on earth to men of good will. Peace, peace
for the nesting whitethroat geese too
in the innermost reaches of Bunnfjord:
they spread their soft breasts over your unborn chicks
in thin eggs, Lord, while
the super-rich on earth race their speedboats towards them:
1900 horsepower
at 220 km per hour are to be unleashed
at the moment when the little whitethroat goslings
new-hatched swim their first clumsy tentative metres
confused by an Earth that whirls round and round your sun,
confused by day and night
and by the circular motions of the moon:
they swim in the waves under your sky,
a sky of sun, of moon, a sky strewn with stars!
And peace, peace to the little ones, when 12
speedboats swoop down on them like arrows in Bunnefjord.
Steer them clear of the young birds, Lord.
Let even the super-rich know goodwill.

*

Yes, *in terra pax hominibus
bonae voluntatis*: peace peace
to the embryo that began to grow in Lisbeth's womb
this night. She's the one with the long plaits who serves
in the watchmaker's shop while the clocks
tick and strike and the pendulums

111

swing in the clocks on the wall and the cuckoo clock
erupts cuck-oo
cuck-oo cuck-oo, she's the one who serves all day long
with lilac nail varnish on fingers and toes
in all this ticking and swinging
in and out and to and fro. Lisbeth
let Jens the salesman undress her last night: when she went out
in the wind that caressed her hips, her thighs, the thin blouse
tight against the young girl's strutting breasts
in the High Street, when she met Jens
there was a kind of sweet itching where the wind caressed
and a warmth grew further in, in her moist entrances.
He had come that morning
with samples of quartz watches and magnifying glasses
from Zeiss, in a pale suit and a wild scent of Hugo aftershave
as he leaned
over the counter. Then he asked her to come to his hotel
for a little drink that evening and she nodded and
disappeared in the wind
home to her bed-sitter where she chose a silk thong
and a blond bra and then
flew off to meet Jens: there was a song

in the young girl's body in the hotel room when Jens undid
her plaits, drew the silk thong down her thighs
and pulled it free of her feet over the lilac-painted
toenails, unfastened
the lacey bra from Lisbeth's slender back
and sank slowly into her wet cunt which opened out
and he came in exultation with thousands of sperm cells in
through her womb and up the Fallopian tube

and left early this morning on the bus to Åndalsnes
while Lisbeth for the very first time arrived late

112

in the watchmaker's shop, as the cuckoo clock crowed 9 times
cuck-oo cuck-oo at her who bore an egg
in the throbbing darkness
of her womb, scarcely 0,2 mm by now, almost invisible
yet in the process of dividing itself
and growing. The bus moves off

with Jens, in blue exhaust fumes. She smiles
shyly

It's as if the springs in all the clocks on the walls
here draw themselves up
around her around Lisbeth: *Laudamus te,*
benedicimus te, adoramus
te, glorificamus te, gratias agimus tibi
propter magnam gloriam tuam Domine Deus,
Rex cælestis, Deus Pater omnipotens. It's as if
they exult with her: a great glory
for Lisbeth in the watchmaker's shop, in the High Street.

Peace peace, for her who becomes an unmarried mother.
Peace peace, for the embryo that is growing. The least
among us, Lord.

Gloria. Gloria. Gloria. Gloria in excelsis Deo.

*

And peace to my old mother of 89 in the clinic:
Domine Fili unigenite, Jesu Christe, Domine Deus,
Agnus Dei, Filius Patris, qui tollis peccata mundi,
miserere nobis qui tollis peccata mundi,

suscipe deprecationem nostram: have mercy on
Mother, there's a flickering in her demented brain.

In my childhood, o God, there were summers of thunder
that hurled darkness over the town of Molde, and
zigzags of lightning that sped
over the meadows of white anemones, and driving rain:
I slipped. Vipers
in every blueberry path, Lord. But no one mentioned

poverty, though the needle in Mother's
mighty Singer sewing machine crackled as it flew
up and down between heaven and earth
patching holes in my trouser-knees,
altering skirts and dresses for my sisters.

Because things weren't so bad in my childhood:
in Mother's house
there were always enough slices of bread, and syrup,
and a hand
that caressed my hair with an infinite gentleness
before I fell asleep under lightning or stars or rain or moon
after night prayer: Now I lay me down to sleep ...

Do you remember? I ask Mother.
'52—that was a winter with snow! 2 metres, at least.
You went with me all the way to school, for I was so small
that only my blue knitted cap emerged above the snow. But
your hand held me tight, you were your snow-plough
through the January snowdrifts even though you carried
my soon-to-be-born sister.

But she doesn't remember. She lies under the white quilt
as though in snowdrifts

and her hands fumble under the pillow
after something she has forgotten.
She does not remember. She looks at me as I sit by her bed
in the clinic, a shadow
glides over her face. Like the shadow
cast by the wing of a big bird.

Not naked, not clothed. Not sick
and not well. She lies
under the white quilt, a snowdrift. Your hand

too is like a bird now. Have you already flown, away
from all of this? This body
that you feel under the quilt—is it yours? Packed
in infants' nappies, a rubber blanket
under the bed-sheet.

You ask whether Mother has come in now
from the barn with fresh milk.
I cannot bring myself to answer that. Grandmother
has lain under turf and cross in Molde graveyard since '52.
I brought some white anemones that I picked for you, I say.
Then a shadow glides over her face a second time, a
big wing moves by her.
She says: I'll take them home to Mother
and Father. It will be dark soon, and I must go home.
You're a kind man, you must bring my greetings
to your parents.
She fumbles under the quilt
and feels an alien
body there, bloated skin and
flesh. Wheelchairs roll

and trays are wheeled
before her eyes, which look
towards the open door. She wants to go home
to Father and Mother and little sister and big brothers

in the white house behind the avenue of cherry-trees
and the green hedge of spruce, up
on the hillside, beyond the mountains
and the blue blue fjord: she does not remember
that they are all long dead. She does not remember
she is a big girl now, that she married in '43, he
was in uniform, there's a war
she has forgotten. She does not remember that this body
gave birth to 3 children, in '44, '45 and '52, that her husband
took off his uniform in '45 and became an office-worker
with many hobbies, a man who went out
every morning and came back for dinner. A tray with food
and pills rolls up to her bed now, she washes it all down.
We'll let her sleep now, says the nurse in sterile
white, a young girl.

I take Mother's hand in mine.
It was you who guided me through the snowy winters.
I can't guide you through this snowdrift here.
We no longer see each other, there is
a flickering between us, a screen that shows
indistinct pictures, incomprehensible words transmitted from
a badly-tuned station. And you have already
set out on your flight.

Over the white house with the cherry avenue
and the green hedge, over the mountains and the blue
blue fjord you are
slowly vanishing.

Qui sedes ad dexteram Patris, miserere nobis. Quoniam tu solus
Sanctus, tu solus Dominus, tu solus Altissimus, Jesu
Christe, cum Sancto Spiritu: in gloria Dei Patris.
Amen.

Credo

Credo in unum Deum ...
I believe in a great God: the nebulae
are the small drops of perspiration in his beard
after the work on all of his creation: yesterday, God, you
created a meadow full of white anemones
above my house, and today you let an anemone girl
whom you created six years ago
come with glowing cheeks, chubby fists clutching
a bouquet. *Anemone nemorosa*: white anemone. For me!
Anemone nemorosa: the white anemone
stands in a glass of water and bears witness to your
creative power, Lord. And this evening you have created
a butterly, *anthocharis cardamines,* that flutters
from the cherry-tree over to the rose-bush that shines
as your lamp in my garden when night comes,
and the roe you made to well out
of the belly of a cod—a *gadus morhua!*—in Lofoten this spring
at 100 metres' depth, hatched only a few weeks later:
you had to guide it out, a tiny fry, to feed on plankton
in the polar waters: *gadus morhua!*
You made this cod pour forth 4 million eggs, more numerous
than all the visible stars, welling out of a belly
in the sea, more numerous than all the sandgrains and ants we can
count! And then you had to go into the woods in Siberia, Lord,
where your foes have left the tree trunks gasping for air
in the poisonous emissions from ovens that remind one
of Babel's tower: there you delivered a she-bear of your created
handiwork. Now a young bear is taking his first steps
under your sun which draws westwards across the sky
and the young bear's eyes see that a moon is kindled and the
mighty Wagon rolls across the vault of heaven. It was you

who created everything, Lord!
And "everything" is only the small drops of perspiration
in your beard. And tonight I dreamed, Lord, that you created
a sacred embryo in my woman's womb, in your image,
by means of my penis in her dark swelling woman's sea, Lord!
An embryo in God's image! You, Lord of things
visible and invisible. Today my woman said: You make
the birds in my heart sing. Those birds too
are created by you, Lord: creator of thrush and
jackdaw, *turdus pilaris* and *picus viridis.* I believe
in you. You are a great God.

Et in unum Dominum Jesum Christum …
The sacred, I think—but the thought stops short
at the sound of my heartbeats in this well-fed body
which goes from special offer to special offer, shows
and lecherous satisfactions.
Now it is evening, I am
a little drunk but not sated, a clock on the wall
strikes the half-hour, a moon
streams in over the floor, the window-frame like a cross. Such simple

symbolism! But the sacred
troubles me, there is something I have switched off, a light
from an angel that always sat in my childhood room and shone
into my dreams, at home with Mother and Father. I am
a guest in this house, it stands on the ridge
like a white dove crouched in a gable
above the town of millennial ruins, in a country
where I grasp only single words of the language,
the house is abandoned, but the owner, my friend,
has given me a key. Now
it will soon be dark, I grope
through this endless room I do not know, glimpse dimly

that it is full
of images of the Virgin with Son, and of the Saviour
on the cross, Jesus' face and Mary
follow me with their dark flaming eyes, as if they lived
there in the frames, on this wall where I only sense
the shadows moving: I believe in the sacred,
but Jesus' face disappeared when I saw all the shows on offer
and lecherous satisfactions in town after town. I
turned my back on him, did he then turn
his back on me? I am unholy, I think, and grope
along the wall for a light-switch. My fingertips
press it down, the light
floods this room and I stare into my own childhood face, as
into a mirror from another time on this wall of sacred,
transfigured faces. And in my heart I hear
the thin voice of a boy who says: Pray for me, Mary.
Sancta Maria, mater Dei, ora pro nobis peccatoribus,
nunc et in hora mortis nostrae. Amen. The spring
in the wall clock scrapes faintly
as it draws itself up to measure out twelve strokes in this room.
Then Jesus' face is suddenly there in the mirror, in the image
which looks at me, endlessly gentle: I am the sacred in you.
Believe in me, and I
am in you. It was for you I was born of the virgin Mary,
for you I suffered under Pontius Pilate, for you I died
on the cross, for you I rose up from the grave. It was
from your grave I rose up, he says. And I look
into the mirror: the traits of my own face! Shining
in his image: he is *Deum de Deo, lumen de lumine,* and
my darkness burns up in his suffering light of love
in this house which sits like a dove in the ridge
above millennial ruins.

Et in Spiritum Sanctum

The language of God vibrates in the prophets' words,
they speak for the wind and the carrion birds
and for Jerusalem's enemies, for crows that pick
in the faded last year's grass in a cold springtime, and for
dead souls. Why is God's face hidden
for us, under heavy layers of dust? We hear
the prophets' words but not

the deep rumbling of the heavenly storm, of distant
lightnings and mountains that shake
in the prophets' voices: God's
sacred wrath—for we do not guard the temple
against Jerusalem's enemies, we play strip-poker
and sell the sacred fatherhood of our children, who
are created in God's image, in return for shares

in big media firms, while our temple is desecrated
and embryos removed from their mothers' wombs and
turned into fragrant ointment on ample female breasts
under thinnest silk. For we do not hear
the language of God which vibrates in the prophets' words,
we do not hear
the gaunt horses neighing by distant churchyards
far away along the sea, in the prophets' voices: death
and judgement are without end at this sea of negligences, we
who could not stay awake, we who could not guard the temple
—even if that were only a little whitewashed chapel
in an inaccessible valley
by a fjord in western Norway. We
who chatter about this and that, while Jerusalem's enemies
desecrate the temple in the night-dark fjords that are our souls!
But there are some
still waiting for a glimpse of God's face: the
wretched in the world, those sick by reason of sin. Frostbitten

121

on the icy windswept plains, burnt by scalding hot springs
they stumble as they make their way over the lava
fields: the flayed, the poor. This,

says the Lord of hosts, is why I loved you
so much that I gave you my only-begotten Son: he
incarnatus est de Spiritu Sancto ex Maria Virgine. We saw

a dove over his head, his eyes were filled with all our yearning
and all the torment of our negligence. The Holy Spirit
was over him like a white bird, when he
was baptized in the river that ran
around the scrawny feet of the prophet; from now on
whoever has eyes shall see God's face
in the Son of Man, and whoever has ears
shall hear his voice, which is mercy,
mercy *in Spiritum Sanctum, Dominum et vivificantem:*
qui ex Patre Filioque procedit, qui cum Patre et Filio
simul adoratur et conglorificatur:
qui locutus est per prophetas.

Et unam, sanctam, catholicam et apostolicam Ecclesiam
All the churches in the world. The high and narrow,
the round and low, the broad: they are the mothers
on earth. In their wombs
human embryos come to birth, at the hands of the fathers
in the sacred water. We return again and again to their bosom
with scraped knees and wounded hearts. The mothers
give us food and drink, while they themselves
sew and hold bazaars and like talking about things small
and exalted, and gossip a little
about each other, and their children, and about the fathers.
The churches in the world are like mother hens,
they peck a little when one of us chicks

strays out of line beyond the farmyard patch,
but draw us in under their wings when danger threatens.

Some are aristocratic and French, like Notre-Dame de Paris:
a real lady with such a long back, who speaks
in a low voice. But her children
are like all the others, stubborn kids who sometimes go astray,
at other times rush in with golden dandelions
for her coffee table, proffered by dirty hands
and pure hearts. Others come from simpler backgrounds, small
windswept chapels on the wide plain
with only the most essential things: a table
with food and drink, chairs to sit on and a fire she keeps
burning for her children when they come in hungry and
thirsty from the hunting trips that start all too early
and it is cold and the winters are endless there.
But there are mothers there, to come home to.
You can believe in them.

I was born by the sea. My mother gave birth to me
in the great days of fishing, the boats came in
with lanterns swinging in the phosphorescence in the nights,
they came into my dreams, brimful of fish,
like thumping hearts.
Father, with his stiffly sloping handwriting and his calculations,
in the evening he went down the hillside, towards the quay.
He came up from the sea with fish in buckets
while I slept under the stars in my attic room by the sea.
When I woke, Mother gave me something to eat, she gave me
milk and honey, she dressed me and taught me to say
"thank you." The church walls were burnt down
and the tower caved in
in the savagery of the War, but Mother was at home,
unshakeable. Afterwards there was only

a simple chapel down near the shore,
but everything one needed was there, just as in
Notre-Dame de Paris. And the drift nets
unfurled like prayers in the dark sea-depths
from small, thumping ships. Mother's heart, Mother's
bosom in this shining milkwhite house, and I played
with my sisters by the endless sea until evening came.

I believe in the church, she is a mother.

Sanctus

King Uzziah, I write. King
Uzziah the leper

died that year. There was no
dial whose hands could be stopped in the hour of his death, no
cogwheel and swinging weights to lock, only sand,
sand that ran down to the bottom of an hourglass.
I creep into the prophet's weatherbeaten sunscorched
leather coat, I, the prophet Isaiah son of Amoz,
I smash the hourglass.

Red sand from an extinct volcano, glass
splinters scattered abroad
in creaking gallows and winds, my vocation
is to stop this time.

King Uzziah who constructed ingeniously conceived
machines of war that stood on towers and the corners
of the wall. They shot out arrows and stones
so that his name flew far and wide like the winds in the world,
and he accepted the homage of 307,500 soldiers. His heart
was filled with arrogance and he marched in all his splendour
into the sanctuary of the Lord

up to the altar of incense where he wanted to burn incense
as only the priests of Aaron's line are permitted to do.
He did not heed the prophet's voice, but when he grew enraged
at the priests, the sickness broke out on his forehead.
Sand ran in his hourglass. Red sand
from an extinct volcano, glass: the fine
trickling sandgrains, an almost imperceptible
stream of dry sand, so thin. I was a witness

125

to almost imperceptible alterations in King Uzziah's face:
the sickness broke out, from the forehead downwards,
with sores and scabs. *Madrosis Superciliorum
et Ciliorum.* The nose fell in and was clogged by cracks
that dropped yellow matter into the nostrils. His voice
became hoarser. On the extremities of the king's body
came many nodes and bumps, sores and *ulcera.*
His hands
and his feet were infiltrated. No feeling from the feet
up to above the knees. The upper eyelids detached by sores.
A reduced ability to close
the eyes, especially the left, where the folds of skin
gradually disappeared, thanks to the sores. The eyeballs
protruded. *Leproma
et Atrophia Iridis cum Synechia posterior Oc. Sin.*

It was in his days, I say, in the profane King Uzziah's days
that the Lord filled me with wrath. From the Lord
God of hosts a voice rings in my ears: Truly, many houses
shall be desolate, great and goodly houses
shall stand empty. The Lord stretches out his hand
against this people who despise the word of the saints
of Israel, he strikes a blow that makes the earth
shake, and corpses lie like refuse and dirt in the streets,
and the light vanishes under heavy clouds on earth.
And because Zion's daughters put on airs
and walk with haughty neck and dart playful glances
and mince along with jingling anklets
the Lord will make their heads scurfy
and he will rip off their shame: the anklets
off, the ornaments in the shape of suns and moons
off, the ear-rings, armbands, veils, belts
off, the finger-rings and nose-rings
off, the sweet perfume rubbed off, their thin undergarments
ripped off.

Then, says the Lord, there will be a rotten stench
instead of fragrance.
There will be a rope
instead of a belt,
a bald pate
instead of artful curls,
sackcloth instead of finery
and branding instead of beauty.
Because they trust in human beings—
who have only breath in their nostrils!—
all they adore shall be thrown to the moles and bats
and you shall flee into caves in the hills and hide yourselves
in mountain crevices.

In the year King Uzziah died, I, Isaiah, the son of Amoz,
saw the Lord sitting on a high, high
royal throne. The train
of his robe filled the temple. Seraphs hovered
around him, each seraph with 6 wings on their glorious angelic
bodies of intellect and light. With two feathery wings
they hid their faces, with two
they hid their feet, and with two wings they flew
between the Lord
and me.
And one called to the other in their angelic language Kadosh
Kadosh Kadosh *Sanctus, Sanctus, Sanctus,* yes Holy Holy
Holy is the Lord God of hosts.
I, Isaiah the son of Amoz, who live in a time of
creaking gallows in wind and in sand, I heard the seraphs say:
All the earth is full of his glory!
Their cries were like thunderstorms in the air, like
jolting earthquakes
and the threshold gates shook when the cry resounded,
and the house I was in
filled with smoke.

Then I said: Wretched, wretched
am I! There is no hope for me
for I am a man of impure lips
and I live among a people of impure lips,
and now my eyes have seen the Lord God of hosts.

Then one of the seraphs flew
out to me, the six-winged angel
held a glowing stone in his hand
taken with tongs from the altar.
He touched my mouth
with the glowing stone and said: See, this
has touched your lips.
Now your misdeed is no more, and your sin
expiated. His voice, from the first angelic circle of intellect
and light, was a storm
as of the giant organs in the mighty cathedrals of future ages
and a balsam that cooled my scorched lips:
Sanctus, Sanctus, Sanctus
Dominus Deus Sabaoth he sang, the highest angel,
Pleni sunt caeli et terra gloria tua: All the earth is full
of His glory.

Then I heard the Lord's voice: Whom shall I send? Who
will be our messenger?

Then I said to the Lord: See, here am I.
Send me. I am Isaiah, son
of Amoz. Your prophet. My lips
are pure. Send me out, I am
the Lord's wind. The word.

The word is to be sent out
It is to be sent across the seven seas

the word is to be sent out across all the centuries
The word is to be sent across all thresholds
It is not the wind that rages in sea in desert sand on thresholds
in windows in chimneys, but the word
The word shall set up gallows
and the word shall let the gallows dangle
The word shall shatter this time of gallows wind sand broken
glass and creaking wheels

The word is to be sent out over the unharvested fields
over poisoned yellow last year's grass
the word is to be sent over children's stolen dolls with
heads torn off and to the desecrated children,
their souls dark ashflakes in the air
The word is to be sent to shows and lecherous
theatrical performances the word
to China where they remove the liver and kidneys
from living prisoners
and to Taiwan's hotel rooms where small boys are bought
for money, their souls like screeching owls
in the night wind and under the crescent moon,
your word, and to the clinics
where embryos are removed from their mothers' wombs
and turned into fragrant ointment
on ample female breasts under thinnest silk.
The word is to be sent out: the language of God vibrates
in my words. The word

The word is to be sent out
For it is not calendar pages that fly
in this wind, it is the word the word that is on its way
For it is not the calendar that turns over our lives
It is the word
which is the stumbling stone the word that supports us

The word: cleave the wood
and there it is, the word
Lift up the stone
and there it is, the word

For unto us a child is born, it is the word
To us a son is given, the word the word
And the government is laid upon his shoulder

For it is not the calendar that turns over
our lives, but the word the word

There is no dial
whose hands can be stopped, no cogwheel
and pendulum weights to lock
in the hour of our death
but sand sand that runs
down to the bottom of an hourglass

which I, the prophet Isaiah, son of Amoz, smash
with the word the word
Glass splinters and sand and the word
For we are born in the hour of our death, in the word
in the word: *Benedictus*
qui venit in nomine Domini
Hosanna in excelsis

Agnus Dei

Agnus Dei, qui tollis peccata mundi:
miserere nobis.
Yes, *miserere* the holy words of the Mass
ring through my brain
here where I stand by Father's grave on the hillside
above a milkwhite fjord in western Norway.
It is late autumn and misty, but this was the time
in the old days for gathering the sheep, Father,

in the wild Øygard mountains. It snowed
on the mountains last night. Soon
winter will creep down here, towards the fjord.
A faint smell of diesel oil
floats up to the graveyard in the evening dark.
You got a proper gravestone, Father, granite
roughhewn like your own self.
I place heather on your grave. My glands can still
recall the taste of heather-honey from your beehives.
And suddenly I see you, in your white beekeeper's clothing
with a swarm in the air, shining
around your head in the evening sun: it must have been
August, when the sun was in the sign of Leo in the vault
of heaven above the town of Molde.
Agnus Dei, qui tollis peccata mundi,
miserere nobis. There are sheep-bells in those words, Father,

and autumn. Heather and lambs. Honey.
And milk. You do not understand the words, and I
do not understand the language of God that tinkles
and rings in me. So we understand
equally little, you who swim through the soil

under the turf here, soon nothing more
than a skull and a tracery of bones,
and I who stand up here in the autumn mist and still wait
to be allowed to swim with you through the earth
towards a mighty resurrection where our bodies are stripped
of all lecherous lust and washed clean
of lies and deceit.

You had mercy on me, Father. You gave me a beating
and the matter was closed—righteous
like the God of Israel.
But there was something
we never managed to say. And now
there's really nothing else to say
than that I will soon be following you. Now this millennium
is rolling towards its end and soon wet snow will come
down here by the fjord on a planet that slowly rotates
on its own axis and circles elliptically round a sun
in the endless universe. You swim and swim
there under the thin crust of soil I stand upon.
I feel dizzy: the planet spins and spins around, it is as if I
lose my footing in this weak wind of stars and
diesel oil. *Miserere*
nobis.

You knew these sciences. We went up the hill,
so red with rowan berries and the twittering of thrushes,
in among the hazel bushes, one autumn
so long ago, we plucked green-brown nuts, up
on the hill where we searched for the sheep, the steep crags.
And suddenly
I slipped and plunged
down a mountainside in the salty air over a scree
and the sea lay infinitely far below me. Until I felt

your grasp: you hauled me in again, like a lamb.
I remember the tinkling, the bells. The sheep
came to us! Their
bleating. I feel the taste of milk and honey
you gave me on the mountain, your hands
like a mother's then. While the great moon
floated up in the skies, you told me,
a nine-year-old child, about scientific numbers

and threw your earth-moist hands about in the air.
We are standing on a sphere
that rolls elliptically round the sun, you said: the earth.
We are flying off at a speed of almost 30 kilometres per second.
But we are far away,
there are 150 million kilometres of universe
between the sun and us. The sheep-bells
tinkled and the honey was sweet in my mouth as you told me
about an earth that turns on an axis
at an angle of 66°33' which points towards
the celestial poles. It is like a mighty
clockwork, you said, here in the Milky Way, you said

out under the autumn sky and you carried me
down the hillside with the sheep playing on their bells
a music of the spheres before us, a *harmonice mundi*
sounded forth over this western fjord through the night
and the endless sky where the mountains danced
under the moon and the planets circled on their paths

around the same, invisible sun that autumn '54,
when Father's hand grasped me like a lamb about to plunge
down high above the town of Molde.

No, Father, I am not homeless in a world of mechanical
energies, particles and rays. I know the taste
of salt that makes its way
in from the sea to this fjord, all the way up to this churchyard
where I stand by your grave: natrium chloride NaCl.
There is a roar of buses and taxis down there,
the smell of diesel and salt. Someone laughs in the hotel.

You never mentioned the Lord's name to me.
You never bowed down before any altar
built by human beings, Father. Your science
was of this world: you pondered sheep and constellations
and the language of bees as you walked over the wild
Øygard mountains through the Sundays of my childhood.
That is the Wagon, you said, and I saw
the heavenly chariot rolling brightly in the autumn evenings:
seven powerful stars, you said. There is a
great arithmetic and geometry in the sky. Look
at the line between the rear wheels
in that chariot that shines out there in the darkness:
if you extended it five times as much in space,
you would reach the Pole star!

I was twelve when I learned about the Wagon
and the lines in your heaven, Lord, I say
to the Lord Sabaoth *Miserere nobis,* yes have mercy
have mercy on Father and me and on all of us
who are familiar with energies, particles and rays, with the salt
that imperceptibly settles on our window panes
out towards the Atlantic,
and with electronic traces, but not with *Agnus Dei*—
I remember the slaughterer's motors that came
and fetched the lambs, I can still recall the harsh
smell of slaughter in my nostrils. The open

doors of the lorries stood like black insects' wings
in the farmyard, while the bells tinkled.
Ding dong and then off in blue exhaust fumes
over the gravel path. The lamb
as sacrifice—that, I understood as a child—
but as victor? And the milk, fresh, brought in a cup
to the lamb in the barn
and the serious child in the mornings.
And the milk in my daughter's breasts,
nine months pregnant.
Miserere, miserere on the unborn child too *miserere!*

Mary, I understand, in my daughter's body, far on
in her pregnancy. But
I cannot understand the dust of the stars
and my father's rotting body, now being stripped
of its flesh (dust, dust),
as anything other than particles and rays, mass and energy, not
the heart of the atom, not
the thoughts in the cells, not the conversations,
the caresses, the sufferings
in the dust, in the soil. (The vocal chords
that quiver in the dust. The dust
that settles on the rope in the attic, the child in the dust
who finds her dangling: mother. The protruding eyes, the blue
face. Dust dust. A shrie
k, dust.) Not the heart of the atom.

And I take up this picture and understand: Mary
and the child. Milk
and honey, sheep and lambs. Ding
dong
tinkles through the whole starry arc of the zodiac, Father!

135

Your grave your
flesh which is being dissolved your dust the child
that is to be born
the beehives brimful of honey: everything swings
as in a mighty clockwork through the zodiac
and spreads itself abroad
over 18° latitude, 9° on the ecliptic's sides
of the heavenly spheres.
Through the earth where you swim, there swings
this mighty wheel of giving birth death and rising up
in exultation. Ding
dong. Ding
dong. It swings even into heaven
with its bees precipitous mountains waterfalls graves
teats full of milk
mother's breasts tinkling sheep and lambs and deserts,
seas volcanoes, with its
barns its car parks its escalators
smallholdings and cathedrals, it swings
dripping with milk and honey from Øygard mountain
between the shining white spiral galaxies
of the Milky Way, Father.
Here are
enough milk and honey, and light!
We are on our way, the bells
tinkle before us, and we glide through the starry arc
of the zodiac, each on his own side
of a crust of soil between earth and heaven: your grave
by the milkwhite Molde fjord, Father. The peace
of God, yes the peace of the Lamb
tinkles through the autumn evening here
where we swing through the universe
in a shining spherical motion.
Agnus Dei, qui tollis peccata mundi,

miserere nobis. Agnus Dei, qui tollis
peccata mundi, miserere nobis. Agnus Dei,
qui tollis peccata mundi,
dona nobis pacem. Ding dong, by your
grave, Father. Ding
dong
and the peace of the Lamb to us all.
The peace of the Lamb.
And over ashes and smoke, glass splinters, distorted
faces in the mirrors *pacem pacem.*

Afterword

Brian McNeil

Knut Ødegård was born in Molde, a small town on the west coast of Middle Norway, in 1945. (In "Credo," he alludes to the parish church in Molde, which burned down in 1940 and was later rebuilt as the Lutheran cathedral.) He studied theology and philology at the University of Oslo and published his first poems *Drøymaren, vandraren og kjelda* ("The dreamer, the wanderer and the spring") in 1967. There are two Norwegian Languages, Nynorsk and Bokmål, and most of Ødegård's literary production is in Nynorsk. He has published ten volumes of poetry and many translations of poems and plays and prose, and he has been translated into numerous languages.

He has written excellent introductions to Iceland. His second wife, the choir director Þorgerður Ingólfsdóttir, is Icelandic, and he has spent many years "commuting" between Iceland and Norway. He was the director of the Scandinavian centre in Reykjavik for a number of years, and he his had a state stipend from Norway since 1989. He has been awarded many prizes and honours, in Norway and in other countries,

The Norwegian word *ildsjel* (literally "soul of fire") might have been coined specifically to describe him: he has the gift of infecting others with the enthusiasms that glow in his own heart. One fruit of this gift is the international literary Bjørnson Festival held in Molde each summer. He founded this in 1992 and has been its active president, becoming honorary president in 2001 (this is the background to a number of his daughter's remarks in the poem "Kyrie").

One is tempted to apply the rather old-fashioned expression "a man of letters" to Knut Ødegård, but this would fail to capture an essential aspect of his activities: it is not only in the field of literature and culture that be is active. He was Consul for Slovakia in two Norwegian counties from 1995 to 1997, and is now General Consul for Macedonia in the whole of Norway—no sinecure during the Kosovo conflict in 1999.

Knut Ødegård became a Catholic in 1992. This raises the question of what he intends when he interweaves his own poems with the texts of the Latin Mass.

The structure of *Missa* has an obvious parallel in Benjamin Britten's *War Requiem* (1962). It has been argued, must recently by Marvyn Cooke (*Britten: War Requiem,* Cambridge University Press, 1966), that the composer's interweaving of the venerable Latin texts with raw, unflinching poems about the brutality of war written by Wilfred Owen, who was killed at the age of twenty-five in France on Armistice Day 1918, is intended to show up the emptiness of the "consolation" that the Christian faith offers to those who suffer. In view of Britten's lifelong pacifism and his attitude to organised Christianity, this interpretation is certainly plausible. In the case of *Missa*, however, there is no reason to doubt that the poet intends his prayers to be taken seriously (see for example the opening of "Gloria").

A second possibility is suggested by the Norwegian publisher on the book's jacket, namely that Ødegård "brings the dark and destructive forces in the human person into the Catholic Mass, which is performed in a space that accommodates all that is human ... here, the dark mysteries and the splintered experiences find an answer in a larger context."

This is doubtless pious, but it reduces Knut Ødegård to an apologist who has nothing deeper to offer sufferers than the classic Christian consolation. This, however, flinches from genuinely accepting the tragic dimension of human life. Innumerable Christian writers have explained away the riddle of suffering by pointing to a "higher" justice, a "higher" intention, a "higher" providence, etc. The attempt to reconcile faith in a loving and almighty God with the brutalities of existence on earth is technically called "theodicy". I may permit myself, as a theologian, the observation that no intellectually or spiritually satisfactory theodicy has ever been proposed. To turn *Missa* into Christian apologetic is to trivialise what the poet is doing. Such an interpretation neuters the tremendous tension that drives these poems, the unbearable discord between the Latin texts (affirmations of faith in a loving Lord) and the Nynorsk texts (e.g. the shriek of the poet's daughter in "Kyrie," or the incomprehensible suffering of his old mother in "Gloria").

As I read *Missa*, Knut Ødegård does something much more interesting than these two alternatives. He refuses to dissolve in some allegedly "higher" harmony the tragedy, the incompleteness, the sheer waste of human life: God's face is genuinely hidden. At the same time, the ancient words of the Mass pulsate through the whole work with their proclamation of the incarnation, the death and resurrection of the one who is "the Lamb of God," and this too is reality! Neither the darkness nor the light is to be denied, and the last words of "Agnus Dei" embrace both realities.

What this means is that *Missa* does not supply an answer to our existential questions. Every answer, whether born of belief or not, would mean an unacceptable simplification of reality. Ødegård does something greater than this: he formulates the questions in such a way that the reader is given a deeper insight both into the mystery of suffering and into the mystery of God's presence. Precisely this is the task of theology: not to take the sting out of our questions, but to formulate them as exactly (and provocatively) as possible. In this perspective, *Missa* is certainly an important theological work!

This essay originally appeared as the Afterword to Missa *upon its first English language publication by Dedalus Press in 2002.*